Relationships, Results, and Refocus

Relationships, Results, and Refocus

A Journey in Educational Leadership

Dr. Wendy Birhanzel
Dr. Rupak Gandhi
Dr. Britney Gandhi

BLOOMSBURY ACADEMIC
NEW YORK • LONDON • OXFORD • NEW DELHI • SYDNEY

BLOOMSBURY ACADEMIC
Bloomsbury Publishing Inc, 1359 Broadway, New York, NY 10018, USA
Bloomsbury Publishing Plc, 50 Bedford Square, London, WC1B 3DP, UK
Bloomsbury Publishing Ireland, 29 Earlsfort Terrace, Dublin 2, D02 AY28, Ireland

BLOOMSBURY, BLOOMSBURY ACADEMIC and the
Diana logo are trademarks of Bloomsbury Publishing Plc

First published in the United States of America 2026

Copyright © Wendy Birhanzel, Rupak Gandhi, and Britney Gandhi, 2026
AASA Logo © The School Superintendents Association (AASA)

Cover images: © istock/DreamerStock, © istock/Turkan Rahimli

All rights reserved. No part of this publication may be: i) reproduced or transmitted in any form, electronic or mechanical, including photocopying, recording or by means of any information storage or retrieval system without prior permission in writing from the publishers; or ii) used or reproduced in any way for the training, development or operation of artificial intelligence (AI) technologies, including generative AI technologies. The rights holders expressly reserve this publication from the text and data mining exception as per Article 4(3) of the Digital Single Market Directive (EU) 2019/790.

Bloomsbury Publishing Inc does not have any control over, or responsibility for, any third-party websites referred to or in this book. All internet addresses given in this book were correct at the time of going to press. The author and publisher regret any inconvenience caused if addresses have changed or sites have ceased to exist, but can accept no responsibility for any such changes.

A catalog record for this book is available from the Library of Congress

ISBN: HB: 979-8-7651-4877-8
PB: 979-8-7651-4876-1
ePDF: 979-8-7651-4878-5
eBook: 979-8-7651-4879-2

Typeset by Integra Software Services Pvt. Ltd.
Printed and bound in the United States of America

For product safety related questions contact productsafety@bloomsbury.com.

To find out more about our authors and books visit www.bloomsbury.com and sign up for our newsletters.

To every educator who has ever questioned whether their presence truly makes a difference in a student's life. Please know that it does. Whether in the quiet act of listening to a child's worry, the daily encouragement of a struggling reader, or the fierce advocacy for equitable policies in your district—your willingness to show up and care transforms lives. To all the students that I have had the honor to know, thank you for allowing me to be part of your journey—you inspire me.
— *Dr. Wendy Birhanzel*

To my incredible family—Britney, Jagger, and Emersen and Tex—thank you for sharing this transformative journey in education with me. Your boundless love and understanding reinforce my belief that a home filled with support and acceptance sets the stage for what's possible in our schools. And to every educator tirelessly seeking solutions for more impactful, student-centered systems: your dedication fuels progress. Keep reimagining, keep innovating, and never lose sight of why we do this work.

In my earliest days teaching special education through Teach for America in Houston, I witnessed how a single caring relationship could radically shift a student's sense of possibility. That lesson continues to guide me—thank you for choosing to show up for our kids every day. — *Dr. Rupak Gandhi*

For the teachers who taught me that compassion and high expectations can—and must—coexist. For the administrators who opened doors for me to stretch my leadership wings. For the countless families who entrusted me with their children's hopes, struggles, and dreams—you shaped my understanding of authentic community partnership. To my own teachers as a student in rural Washington State to the many educators I have had the privilege to work with: thank you for choosing to show up every day for our kids. — *Dr. Britney Gandhi*

For my loving family—Mom, Dad, and Marcos—thank you for helping me realize I have leadership within me. To the teachers who believed my passions will reach above the stars—you helped me realize a journey can't rely on yourself. To all the programs-Harrison School District 2 Board of Education, GenYOUth, and Peak Education—thank you for allowing my morals and values reach far nationally/locally. After all, I trust the connections I made throughout my journey because Jesus Christ knew these people will only help me grow. At the end of the day, I am grateful for the negatives and the positives, as it only helped me advance.... Thank you. —*Aidan Gallegos*

To Fargo Public Schools—whose guidance transformed my doubts into milestones—and to my teachers, mentors, family, and God, for making every learning opportunity unforgettable.
—*Zahabu Christine*

"True leadership in education is born not just from vision, but from the courage to listen, the dedication to nurture, and the resolve to transform. Leadership that fails to include student voices fails to grasp the essence of its mission."

— *Paraphrased from the author's collective experiences*

Contents

Preface xi

Introduction 1

Prologue: Student Reflections 3

Part 1 Relationships 7

1 Building Strong Foundations 11

2 Embracing Growth Mindsets 19

3 Nurturing Trust and Communication 27

4 Empowering Student Voice 35

5 Community Engagement and Collaboration 41

6 Creating Inclusive Spaces for All 49

Reflections: HSD2 Student Author Reflections (Aidan Gallegos) 57

Part 2 Results 61

7 Strategic Alignment and Systems Thinking 65

8 Governance and School Board's Role 71

9 Operational Planning and Cascading Goals 83

10 Strategic Staff Alignment 93

11 Decision-Making, Strategic Decision-Making, and Strategic Execution 99

12 Culture of Improvement and Reflection 107

13 Broader Educational Leadership Considerations 115

Reflections: FPS Student Author (Zahabu Christine) 125

Part 3 Refocus 131

14 The Leadership Time Dilemma 135

15 Defining What Matters Most 143

16 Delegation and Empowerment 151

17 Leveraging Technology and AI 159

18 Creating Space for Reflection and Strategic Thinking 165

19 The Ripple Effect of Reclaimed Time 171

20 Collective Call to Action 179

Bibliography 181

Preface

In the field of education, each day is an opportunity to make a meaningful difference in the lives of students, educators, and communities. For those who choose the path of educational leadership, the journey is filled with complex challenges, rewarding connections, and an unwavering dedication to fostering environments where every student can thrive. *Relationships, Results, and Refocus: A Journey in Educational Leadership* captures this path, presenting a vision of leadership that is as reflective as it is practical, as student-centered as it is systems focused.

This book was born from our shared experiences as educational leaders who have spent countless nights wondering how best to lift up every student. From designing equity-focused policies to meeting with families long after the final bell, we've seen how urgent it is to align leadership choices with student voices. Each chapter weaves together insights on building strong relationships, achieving measurable results, and cultivating a mindset of continuous improvement. In an era marked by rapid change and growing complexities, these three pillars—relationships, results, and refocus—serve as vital touchstones, guiding leaders in creating supportive, inclusive, and effective learning environments.

In *Relationships, Results, and Refocus: A Journey in Educational Leadership*, we—Wendy Birhanzel, Rupak Gandhi, and Britney Gandhi—combine our experiences as educational leaders to share a collective narrative. Each of us brings a unique perspective shaped by our journeys: Wendy and Rupak as 2023 State Superintendents of the Year from Colorado and North Dakota, and Britney as a rural district superintendent balancing the demands of leadership and innovation in smaller communities. Together, the authors aim to provide a diverse and holistic lens on educational leadership. This book is not just a reflection of our journeys through the varied landscapes of Colorado, North Dakota, and rural America; it is a manifesto centered on the belief that students must always remain at the heart of leadership.

Introducing Our Three Authors

Dr. Wendy Birhanzel

Wendy's educational tenure began as a teacher in South Central Los Angeles. Always fascinated by the way trust and empathy can propel students forward, Wendy pursued multiple roles—teacher, instructional coach, principal, district leader—before becoming superintendent of Harrison School District Two in Colorado. Her leadership focuses on bridging achievement gaps, fostering staff collaboration, and upholding equity. Wendy's experiences formed the basis of her understanding that true change hinges on authentic relationships and the unwavering belief in every student's potential while demonstrating that zip code does not define success.

Dr. Rupak Gandhi

Rupak's background is deeply tied to educational justice. Raised with a keen awareness of social inequities, he joined Teach for America in Houston to make a tangible difference. He taught elementary special education, discovering how an inclusive mindset can transform learning for students with unique needs. He vividly recalls working with Bianca, a student in the life-skills program who was higher functioning than initially recognized. As a special education resource teacher, Rupak pushed into her services each day and witnessed Bianca's remarkable growth when the right supports were in place—watching her blossom into a more confident and engaged learner confirmed that every student can thrive in an inclusive environment.

This early experience fueled his passion for equity-driven leadership. Rising through principalships and district administration, Rupak eventually became superintendent in Fargo, North Dakota, championing reforms that foreground student voice in strategic planning. His perspective merges real-world classroom insights with a district-wide lens of accountability and justice.

Dr. Britney Gandhi

Raised in rural Washington State, Britney grew up watching her local community rally support for schools when increased funding was needed.

She, too, joined Teach for America in Houston, teaching high school ESL and ELA. Working with ESL students was brand new to her, and she was inspired by the stories her intermediate ESL students wrote about how they immigrated to the United States. Some of their treks were so arduous; they were simply grateful to be in the United States despite the challenges they then faced. Seeing firsthand the resilience of English learners sparked her dedication to culturally responsive teaching and leadership. Progressing into district leadership roles, Britney embraced the challenges of smaller, more rural school systems, focusing on innovation, relationship-building, and reflective practices that honor both staff well-being and student growth. Her story illustrates that no matter the size of the district, the core principles of empowerment, trust, and intentional reflection matter most.

A Mantra for Student-Centered Leadership

What makes this book distinct is our unwavering commitment to amplify student voices. Truly effective educational leadership requires not only making decisions with students in mind but actively listening to their insights, experiences, and feedback. After all, students are the ultimate recipients of every policy, initiative, and action taken by school and district leaders. By incorporating their reflections throughout this book, the authors hope to illustrate how student voices provide clarity and direction, guiding leaders to create systems that are responsive, equitable, and impactful.

A Deep Respect for Student Voice

At the heart of this book is a profound respect for student voice. Our own experiences have consistently shown that authentic leadership emerges when the perspectives of those most directly impacted—students—are welcomed and amplified. In these pages, you will find reflections from current students and recent graduates who have experienced firsthand the impact of our work. By spotlighting these voices, we aim to offer not just our own insights, but a broader understanding of how leadership choices resonate with those we serve.

Whether we are shaping a district-wide strategic plan or reimagining daily classroom practices, placing students at the center is not a platitude—it is the essence of our approach. Student authors Aidan and Zahabu remind us that educational systems are not static; they evolve when students speak up and leaders embrace their honest feedback.

Why Embrace Reflection?

Reflections from our student authors serve as a call to remain open, resilient, and ever evolving as leaders. In education, our learning never ends. These reflections underscore the importance of self-awareness, adaptability, and humility, reminding us that every experience offers a lesson, and every challenge brings growth—a notion we strive to teach our students daily. Whether we are rethinking discipline policies or overhauling curriculum, it is often the open-minded capacity to "refocus" on what matters most that sparks true innovation.

A Call to Shared Purpose

Leadership is not a one-size-fits-all journey. While our paths may differ, we share a common mission: to serve students and communities with integrity, intention, and purpose. This book is our contribution to that mission, a resource for leaders seeking to navigate the complexities of education while keeping students at the center of every decision.

As you read our book, we invite you to reflect on the voices of our students, consider the strategies presented, and adapt the lessons that resonate most deeply with you. Together, we can create a more responsive and equitable educational system—one that empowers every student to succeed. We challenge you, as an educator or stakeholder, to adopt the bold stance that tomorrow's success stories depend on our willingness to listen, adapt, and refocus on what truly matters.

Thank you for joining us on this journey. We look forward to learning with you and from you, as we collectively push the boundaries of what educational leadership can and should be.

— Wendy, Rupak, Britney, Aidan, and Zahabu

Introduction

The intention with *Relationships, Results, and Refocus* is to equip, inspire, and support educational leaders who share the authors' dedication to making a positive, lasting impact. The authors hope that the ideas, strategies, and reflections presented provide readers with renewed clarity, fresh perspectives, and actionable guidance as they navigate their own journeys in educational leadership.

Educational leaders stand at an intersection of promise and responsibility. The choices they make—how time is spent, whom to include in decision-making, and how to balance accountability with empathy—can shape not just individual student experiences but the trajectory of entire communities. Readers are invited to join this commitment: to lead with purpose, inspire with integrity, and serve with heart.

The intent of this book is not to provide all the answers but to share actionable strategies that leaders can adapt to their unique contexts. The brevity of each chapter—though supplemented with deeper anecdotes—remains intentional, offering clear, practical insights that inspire reflection and implementation rather than overwhelm. By sharing their experiences and lessons learned, the authors aim to spark dialogue and encourage other leaders to contribute their own perspectives to the collective conversation about educational leadership.

Each part of the book begins with the authors' perspectives and concludes with a reflective response from a student who has experienced the systems they lead. This format ensures that the ideas shared are grounded in the realities of those served and reinforces the belief that student voices are a powerful catalyst for meaningful change. By pairing leadership strategies with student reflections, the book fosters deeper understanding and inspires action, showcasing not just the theory of leadership but its lived effects in hallways, classrooms, cafeterias, and beyond.

The book is organized into three parts, each reflecting a critical pillar of educational leadership: relationships, results, and refocus. Each section builds upon the last, offering a comprehensive exploration of the practices that drive meaningful change.

The first section highlights the foundational importance of trust and connection within school systems. Wendy Birhanzel explores how strong relationships foster collaboration and support student success, delving into case studies, personal anecdotes, and research on how empathy, clear communication, and community partnerships elevate school culture. Student reflections reveal the profound impact these connections have on academic and personal journeys.

The second section examines how leaders can align resources, time, and energy to achieve measurable outcomes. Rupak Gandhi explores the complexities of strategic alignment, offering practical advice for navigating the challenges of leadership while prioritizing excellence and equity. Through systems thinking and data-informed planning, this section discusses how to set clear goals that reflect both local context and universal standards. Students share how these strategies have tangibly impacted their learning experiences.

The final section addresses the transformative power of reflection and intentionality in leadership. Britney Gandhi discusses how leaders can reclaim their time, leverage tools like AI, and prioritize strategic thinking to create balance and clarity. She underscores the reality of juggling multiple roles—professional obligations, family commitments, and community responsibilities—while maintaining personal well-being.

The authors also acknowledge the significant role Artificial Intelligence (AI) played in shaping this book. Leveraging AI allowed them to focus on the ideas and experiences they wanted to share while enhancing precision and efficiency in the writing process. As advocates for innovation, they believe AI holds tremendous potential for transforming educational systems by bridging equity gaps, improving efficiency, and creating new opportunities for student success. Embracing the possibilities technology offers, they encourage others to do the same. From scheduling software that frees administrators to focus on instruction to adaptive learning platforms that tailor lessons to each student, AI can be a game-changer—when implemented thoughtfully.

Prologue
Student Reflections

We, the student authors in this book, reflect on our journey of growth and learning and acknowledge the profound impact that writing and storytelling have had on our lives. Through the process of crafting their chapters for this book, we have discovered the cathartic power of putting our thoughts and emotions into words, allowing us to process our experiences and make sense of the world around us.

We provide a candid and thought-provoking glimpse into the mind of students navigating their educational journeys within their respective school systems. These reflections serve as windows into the experiences, challenges, and triumphs of young learners as they interact with the diverse academic, social, and personal development opportunities available to us.

With unfiltered honesty and raw vulnerability, we share our perspectives on the dynamic landscape of education. We offer nuanced insights into the effectiveness of teaching methods, the relevance of curriculum content, and the impact of school culture on our overall growth and well-being. Through our narratives, readers are invited to step into the shoes of young authors, witnessing firsthand the joys and struggles of learning, the moments of inspiration and frustration, and the profound transformations that occur within the crucible of education.

Each reflection is a testament to the power of student voice and agency in shaping the educational landscape. As young authors, we wield pens as instruments of change, challenging conventional wisdom, questioning established norms, and advocating for a more inclusive, equitable, and student-centered approach to learning. Our words reverberate with authenticity and passion, demanding attention and action from all stakeholders in the education community.

As readers delve deeper into our student reflections, they are confronted with the complexities and contradictions inherent in the educational experience. They witness the struggles of students grappling with self-doubt and imposter syndrome, the triumphs of those who defy expectations and break barriers, and the untapped potential of every young mind eager to learn and grow.

The reflections offer a poignant examination of the multifaceted nature of education in the modern world. From discussions on the intersection of technology and learning to explorations of cultural identity and representation in the curriculum, we delve into the heart of pressing issues that shape our educational experiences. We confront the challenges of standardized testing, the equity gaps in access to resources, and the need for more diverse voices and perspectives in the classroom.

Through our writing, we not only express our own truths but also challenge readers to reconsider their assumptions about education and the role of young voices in shaping its future. We highlight the importance of fostering a supportive and empowering environment where every student feels seen, heard, and valued for their unique perspectives and lived experiences. In doing so, we inspire a reimagining of education as a collaborative, dynamic, and inclusive journey toward growth and understanding.

As student authors, writing has become a sanctuary, a safe space where we can unravel the complexities of our thoughts and emotions, laying bare their vulnerabilities and fears on the page. In a society that often undervalues the voices of young people, writing has become a radical act of resistance, a means of asserting our truths and reclaiming our narratives.

The act of writing has not only served as a form of self-expression but has also been a vehicle for personal transformation. Through the act of storytelling, we have unearthed hidden depths within ourselves, confronting our own biases, fears, and prejudices. Writing has forced us to reckon with own privileges and biases, challenging us to confront uncomfortable truths and expand our perspectives.

Moreover, we recognize the privilege we have in being able to share our stories and perspectives with a wider audience. We understand that not all young people are given the same opportunities to express themselves and have their voices heard. This realization has only strengthened our commitment to advocating for inclusivity, equity, and social justice in our communities.

Through this collaborative project, we have not only honed their writing skills but have also developed a sense of empathy and understanding for those whose experiences may differ from our own. We have learned to listen deeply to others' stories and to appreciate the diversity of human experiences that exist within our schools and beyond.

In our reflections, we express a sense of gratitude for the guidance and support we have received from our teachers, mentors, and fellow classmates throughout this writing journey. We recognize that it is through the collective effort and encouragement of a caring community that we have been able to grow and succeed in bringing our stories to life.

In the end, our Student Author Reflections stand as a testament to the resilience, creativity, and courage of the next generation of thinkers, dreamers, and change-makers. Through our words, we offer a glimpse of the future—a future shaped by youthful bold vision, unwavering determination, and relentless pursuit of excellence in education and beyond.

As we look toward the future, we are filled with optimism and a renewed sense of purpose. We are eager to continue using our voices to advocate for positive change and to inspire others to share their own narratives. This book is not just a culmination of our writing efforts but a testament to the power of young voices coming together to create a more inclusive and compassionate world.

—Aidan and Zahabu

Part 1
Relationships

In the realm of educational leadership, the foundation upon which educational leaders build their efforts and aspirations is invariably the quality and depth of their relationships. This foundational aspect encompasses not just the connections they foster among colleagues and within communities but also, and crucially, the relationships nurtured with and between students. In this section, the text explores the multifaceted dimensions of relationships within the educational sphere, beginning with an insightful examination of "Building Strong Foundations" and extending through to the creation of "Inclusive Spaces for All." The chapters in this section illuminate the critical importance of relationships from various perspectives and illustrate how they serve as the bedrock of lasting, positive change in schools.

The opening focus on building strong foundations in relationships reveals that trust, respect, and collaboration underpin the success and longevity of all interpersonal connections within an educational context. Here, clear communication and active listening emerge as pivotal tools for nurturing these relationships, enabling educators and leaders to create environments where every individual feels valued, heard, and empowered to contribute to the collective well-being and success of the educational community. Beyond a mere exchange of information, effective communication fosters a sense of belonging, which in turn motivates teachers, staff, and students to invest wholeheartedly in shared goals. Research in organizational psychology supports this view, showing that teams with high trust and open lines of communication tend to achieve better outcomes, from improved student performance to greater teacher satisfaction.

Building upon this foundation, the concept of growth mindsets underscores the transformative power of embracing challenges, persisting through setbacks, and viewing failures as opportunities for reflection and development. While the growth mindset concept initially gained prominence in relation to students' academic mindsets, it is equally vital for teachers, administrators, and other members of the educational community. When educators commit to continuous improvement—recognizing that their own skills, methods, and perceptions can evolve—they model resilience and curiosity for their students. This ethos of lifelong learning helps dismantle rigid hierarchies between teachers and learners, fostering a culture of mutual respect, encouragement, and shared growth. As a result, the teacher-student dynamic matures into a partnership where all parties feel empowered to explore, experiment, and learn from mistakes.

As the exploration continues, nurturing trust and communication becomes a central theme, highlighting the indispensable link between these elements and their cumulative impact on establishing a cohesive, supportive school culture. Trust is often described as the cornerstone of effective educational leadership, and for good reason: without it, even the best-laid strategic plans can fall apart. Trust nurtures collaboration, promotes meaningful professional dialogue, and strengthens relationships beyond the classroom walls to encompass parents, guardians, and the wider community. Clear, empathetic communication—whether in staff meetings, parent conferences, or student assemblies—further cements this trust, ensuring that people not only feel informed but also genuinely included in the educational process.

In addressing the imperative of empowering student voice, this section underscores the importance of recognizing and valuing the unique perspectives and contributions of students. This chapter champions co-constructing knowledge and fostering a learning environment that not only listens to but actively involves students in shaping their educational journeys. By giving students a platform to express ideas, engage in problem-solving, and influence decisions that affect them, leaders create a more inclusive, responsive, and engaging learning experience. Students who feel heard tend to exhibit greater motivation, resilience, and willingness to participate, ultimately leading to deeper learning and stronger connections with their schools.

The narrative then extends into community engagement and collaboration, where the symbiotic relationship between educational institutions and the broader communities they serve takes center stage. Models such as the Collective Impact framework illustrate how cross-sector partnerships can enhance educational outcomes, addressing systemic challenges through a shared vision and aligned actions. By uniting businesses, nonprofit organizations, government agencies, and local community members, schools can broaden their support systems. Such collaborations benefit not only students—who gain access to enriched resources and real-world learning opportunities—but also families and educators, who become part of a larger ecosystem working in unison for educational success.

Finally, creating inclusive spaces for all brings into focus the paramount importance of inclusivity in education. This chapter serves as a call to action for educators to actively dismantle barriers to inclusion and to advocate for equity, diversity, and social justice within and beyond the classroom walls. Inclusive education is not merely about accommodating different backgrounds, identities, or abilities; it is about celebrating them. Schools that purposefully welcome and honor the diversity of their student populations tend to cultivate more innovative, empathetic, and harmonious environments. Moreover, inclusive practices—ranging from differentiated instruction to culturally responsive pedagogy—can help narrow achievement gaps and foster a sense of belonging for all learners.

In sum, Part I: Relationships sets the stage for a profound exploration of the intricate and dynamic connections that form the essence of effective educational leadership. By delving into the principles of trust, respect, communication, growth mindsets, student empowerment, community collaboration, and inclusivity, the discussion reveals how each element is interwoven, creating an environment where every member of the educational community feels connected, respected, and empowered to contribute to a collective vision of success and well-being. These chapters together underscore that relationships, in all their forms, are not a peripheral concern; they are the very heart of what makes a school flourish. When leaders prioritize building and maintaining healthy relationships, they lay the groundwork for sustainable improvements in teaching, learning, and the overall school climate—ultimately shaping an educational experience that values and uplifts every individual.

1 Building Strong Foundations

Building strong foundations in any relationship is essential to its success and longevity. Much like a sturdy building that depends on a solid base, educational relationships similarly thrive on carefully laid cornerstones of trust, respect, and collaboration. In the context of schools and districts, these foundational elements extend beyond just teacher-student interactions; they encompass relationships among peers, administrators, families, and the wider community. By emphasizing clear communication, active listening, inclusive practices, and proactive policies, educational leaders can set the stage for the growth and well-being of every learner.

Why Strong Foundations Matter

The impact of strong relational foundations in education is profound. Research on school climate consistently shows that when students feel supported and valued, they are more likely to attend regularly, engage with learning, and persevere in the face of challenges. Likewise, when teachers sense trust and respect from both their administrators and students' families, they report higher job satisfaction and are more motivated to innovate and collaborate. Moreover, strong relationships contribute to a positive feedback loop: a school with a welcoming culture tends to attract and retain dedicated staff, who in turn invest more energy in nurturing student success.

Clear Communication: The Cornerstone of Connection

One key aspect of building strong foundations is clear communication. Open lines of communication among students, teachers, administrators, and families ensure that everyone feels both heard and valued. It is essential to go beyond mere surface-level exchanges and actively engage in meaningful dialogues that delve into the thoughts, feelings, and experiences of each individual.

While newsletters, emails, or announcements can disseminate information, these avenues are often one-way. To create real connection, leaders need interactive platforms—such as forums, listening sessions, or staff "town halls"—that invite participation and open the door to new ideas. When staff and students feel safe to speak up—knowing their perspectives will not be belittled or dismissed—they are more likely to offer candid feedback. This climate of openness can reveal blind spots and catalyze constructive changes.

Student-Centered Communication

Students, especially those who are shy or feel marginalized, benefit immensely from having multiple channels to voice concerns—whether through digital surveys, anonymous suggestion boxes, or small-group meetings. By fostering a culture of open and honest communication, educators can create an environment where students feel empowered to express themselves, ask questions, and seek guidance without fear of judgment.

Active Listening: The Flip Side of Effective Communication

Effective communication also entails active listening. It is not enough to simply convey information; leaders and teachers alike must be attentive to the messages conveyed by others. Active listening demonstrates empathy, understanding, and a genuine interest in another person's point of view.

Rather than waiting for a speaker to finish so one can respond, truly listening means hearing the emotional undertones and asking clarifying questions.

This attentiveness fosters trust and can de-escalate tensions, preventing misunderstandings that might otherwise snowball. By practicing active listening, educators and administrators model the same empathy and respect they hope students will display among their peers. This cycle of "listen, clarify, respond" enhances rapport and strengthens the human bonds that underpin all successful educational ventures.

Techniques such as paraphrasing ("What I'm hearing you say is … ") and reflective questioning ("Could you elaborate on how that made you feel?") make students and staff feel genuinely heard. These small efforts go a long way in cultivating goodwill and shared respect. Another crucial element of building strong foundations is establishing clear expectations and boundaries. This requires communicating guidelines for behavior, interactions, and academic standards in a consistent and fair manner.

Consistency Builds Trust

Students often look for consistency in how rules are enforced and how praise is delivered. When they see teachers and administrators upholding the same standards for everyone, they feel the environment is just and equitable. This sense of fairness fosters a deeper loyalty and willingness to comply.

When expectations are explicit—such as outlining the goals for a group project or clarifying the steps of a discipline policy—students and staff feel anchored by a sense of purpose. Academic rigor becomes more attainable when learners know exactly what is expected and receive ongoing feedback toward meeting those targets.

Boundaries also help maintain a harmonious atmosphere where everyone's rights and responsibilities are upheld. For instance, specifying protocols for classroom discussions or departmental meetings sets a respectful tone, ensuring people do not talk over one another or dismiss differing viewpoints.

Fostering a Positive School Culture

Building strong foundations in education involves more than just clear communication and explicit expectations; it also requires creating a positive school culture that values diversity, inclusivity, and collaboration. A climate where every individual feels respected and valued for their unique contributions is far more conducive to learning and growth than one steeped in hierarchy or competition.

Celebrating the richness of cultural backgrounds, personal experiences, and diverse perspectives helps create a sense of belonging. This cultural responsiveness not only benefits students academically but also promotes social-emotional well-being for everyone. School leaders who prioritize inclusivity and equality send a strong message that every learner matters. By modeling mutual respect, they encourage staff to do the same, perpetuating a positive cycle that permeates classrooms, hallways, and extracurricular activities.

When students see their identities affirmed and their voices included, they become active participants in shaping school culture. Teachers, too, feel greater ownership of programs and curricula when they are invited into decision-making processes that genuinely respect their expertise.

Strengthening Peer-to-Peer Relationships

Building strong foundations in education also involves nurturing robust relationships not only between students and teachers but among peers. Students who form healthy peer relationships learn teamwork, empathy, and social skills that are critical for life beyond school. Group projects, discussion circles, and peer tutoring systems can enrich academic content, simultaneously teaching students accountability and respect for others' viewpoints.

Encouraging students to see one another as resources, rather than competitors, fosters a sense of communal learning. This can be particularly powerful in classrooms with mixed abilities or diverse backgrounds, as peers learn to appreciate each other's strengths. By developing supportive peer networks, educators can reduce social isolation, minimize bullying, and encourage shared responsibility for the learning environment. Students who feel connected to their classmates are more likely to attend school consistently and actively contribute in class.

Building strong foundations in education is a multifaceted process that demands clear communication, active listening, explicit expectations, a positive school culture, and robust peer relationships. By prioritizing these core elements, educators lay the groundwork for an inclusive, engaging, and empowering learning environment—one that supports both academic achievement and personal growth.

A school community grounded in these values sees benefits on multiple levels: students excel academically, staff collaborate more effectively, and families build stronger trust in the institution's mission. Moreover, this foundation fuels lifelong learning and continuous improvement, as each member of the educational ecosystem feels valued, inspired, and supported.

Building strong foundations is never a one-and-done endeavor; it requires ongoing reflection, adaptation, and dialogue. As you move through the following chapters—whether discussing growth mindsets, nurturing communication, empowering student voice, or fostering inclusivity—you will see how each layer of relationship-building amplifies the next. By anchoring our efforts in trust, respect, and collaboration, educators forge a sustainable platform where all members of the educational family can thrive academically, socially, and emotionally.

When students trust their teachers and feel respected, they exhibit higher motivation and self-efficacy, leading to improved test scores, project outcomes, and overall academic growth. A culture of trust and respect not only benefits individual achievement but also contributes to a positive school climate, where mutual respect and open communication reduce conflict, promote well-being, and encourage supportive relationships among students, staff, and families.

Strong foundations also foster professional collaboration, ensuring that teachers, counselors, and support staff feel comfortable sharing resources and ideas. With clear expectations and open lines of communication, teamwork flourishes, creating an environment where collective expertise enhances instructional practices and student support. This collaborative culture naturally strengthens effective problem-solving, enabling teams to proactively address challenges, identify root causes, and implement sustainable solutions rather than resorting to quick fixes.

Beyond academic and professional benefits, a strong foundation cultivates a sense of belonging for both students and staff. When individuals feel connected to their school environment, student engagement rises, dropout rates decrease, and teacher retention improves. This deep sense of connection fuels empowerment and agency, encouraging individuals at every level—from students to administrators—to voice concerns, suggest innovations, and contribute meaningfully to decision-making. Ultimately, a well-built foundation supports a thriving school community, where growth, collaboration, and continuous improvement become the norm.

Strategies to Build Strong Foundations

Below are practical steps that different stakeholders can take to reinforce these crucial relational underpinnings:

For Students

- Buddy Systems: Implement a buddy system where older students mentor younger ones, helping them adjust to the school environment and feel supported.
- Social Skills Programs: Introduce curricula that teach effective communication, conflict resolution, and empathy—building emotional intelligence and positive social interactions.
- Inclusive Practices: Ensure that classroom routines and school policies are inclusive, making all students feel welcomed, regardless of background or ability.
- Active Listening: Encourage students to practice listening to peers' thoughts and concerns, reinforcing a culture of empathy and understanding.

For Teachers

- Personal Greetings: Greet students by name as they enter the classroom, sending the message that each individual is valued and recognized.
- Consistency and Fairness: Uphold discipline and grading practices that reflect fairness, building trust and mutual respect.
- Student Voice and Choice: Involve students in curriculum planning, feedback loops, and lesson design, giving them ownership of their learning experiences.
- Community Circles: Hold regular community circles or advisory sessions to discuss issues, share ideas, and build rapport among students and staff.

For Administrators

- Inclusive Decision-Making: Involve teachers, staff, and students in major decisions through surveys, committees, and open forums. This transparency fosters a sense of shared purpose.
- Peer Support and Mentorship: Establish support or mentorship programs among staff, encouraging professional growth and collaborative problem-solving.
- Regular Feedback and Recognition: Offer timely, constructive feedback to teachers and staff while acknowledging their contributions, efforts, and achievements.
- Address Bullying and Discrimination: Create clear policies against bullying, harassment, and discrimination, and take proactive measures to protect and affirm every member of the community.

Building strong foundations in education is essential for fostering trust, collaboration, and long-term success. Just as a sturdy structure depends on a solid base, educational relationships thrive when built on clear communication, active listening, and a culture of inclusivity. Strong relational foundations extend beyond student-teacher interactions, encompassing peer relationships, administrator support, and family and community engagement. This chapter explores how intentional strategies—such as fostering open dialogue, setting clear expectations, and prioritizing equity—contribute to a positive school climate where students feel valued, teachers feel supported, and collaboration flourishes. When these foundational elements are in place, academic achievement, staff morale, and overall school culture improve. By investing in meaningful connections and reinforcing shared expectations, educational leaders create an environment where learning, growth, and success become sustainable for all.

2 Embracing Growth Mindsets

In the ever-evolving world of education, the imperative to establish a culture of continuous growth and learning has become increasingly clear. Each school and district faces dynamic challenges—ranging from shifting standards and technological advancements to student diversity and societal changes—that demand an adaptable approach. This chapter explores the significance of fostering a growth mindset among teachers, students, and administrators, emphasizing the multifaceted benefits that come with embracing a mindset centered on progress, resilience, and development.

Why Growth Mindsets Matter in Education

At the heart of building a culture of continuous growth and learning is the concept of growth mindset, popularized by psychologist Carol Dweck. This perspective posits that individuals who believe their abilities and intelligence can be developed through effort and persistence are more likely to achieve success than those with a fixed mindset, who see ability as static. In an educational setting, growth mindset goes beyond simple encouragement; it shapes instructional strategies, assessment methods, and the broader school climate.

A sustained commitment to growth mindsets influences every level of an educational community. Students learn to view mistakes not as dead ends but as opportunities to refine their approaches. Teachers adopt reflective, research-based practices to improve instruction and support diverse learners. Administrators model risk-taking and champion professional development, fostering an environment where staff feel safe to innovate and learn from setbacks.

The Profound Benefits for Students

A key reason to cultivate growth mindsets is the transformative impact on students. When educators encourage learners to embrace challenges, persist in the face of difficulties, and see errors as steppingstones rather than failures, they promote a sense of agency and self-efficacy. Research has shown that students who develop this mindset often outperform their fixed-mindset peers academically, as they are more likely to engage in deep learning, set higher personal goals, and persevere.

Growth mindset environments emphasize the intrinsic joy of discovery. Students learn to relish the process of exploration and adapt their strategies when obstacles arise. This intrinsic motivation can lead to higher-quality work and more consistent effort. By framing challenges as opportunities for growth, learners become comfortable stepping outside of their comfort zones. Whether tackling advanced math problems or experimenting in a science lab, students with growth mindsets tend to view risk-taking as part of a natural learning curve.

Beyond academic success, the skills nurtured by a growth mindset—critical thinking, resilience, and adaptability—prepare students to navigate personal, professional, and societal challenges throughout their lives. As technology and job markets continue to evolve, these skills become increasingly vital for long-term success.

Students who internalize the growth mindset often engage in goal setting, progress monitoring, and self-correction. They build metacognitive awareness, learning how to learn, which is critical for higher education, careers, and personal pursuits. This self-direction paves the way for autonomy and leadership, equipping them to thrive in a rapidly changing global landscape.

Empowering Teachers Through a Growth Mindset

For teachers, committing to a growth mindset involves lifelong learning and professional development. Teaching is a complex, ever-changing profession. New technologies, shifting curricula, and evolving student needs mean no teacher's skill set remains static.

Reflective Practices

By regularly analyzing their own methods, gathering feedback from colleagues, and staying current on educational research, teachers can refine their approaches over time. Reflection empowers them to address skill gaps in instructional design or classroom management before they become entrenched habits.

Professional Collaboration

Growth-minded educators actively seek mutual support. Whether through peer observations, co-teaching arrangements, or professional learning communities (PLCs), collaboration amplifies individual efforts, as teachers share strategies, challenges, and successes.

Mentorship and Ongoing Training

When schools facilitate mentorship programs, new or struggling teachers can learn from experienced colleagues. Meanwhile, ongoing training—ranging from workshops on new technology tools to seminars on culturally responsive teaching—enables continuous adaptation. This culture of learning models the same growth mindset expected from students, ensuring alignment between classroom practices and institutional values.

Teacher Agency

Growth mindset also fosters teacher agency. If educators feel free to experiment, reflect on outcomes, and adjust strategies, they develop a stronger sense of ownership over their practice. This autonomy can boost morale and encourage creative problem-solving in meeting the diverse needs of their students.

The Administrator's Role in Shaping Growth Cultures

Administrators—principals, district officials, and superintendents—play a pivotal role in shaping the culture of continuous growth and learning throughout a school community. Their influence spans policies, resource allocation, and the tone of day-to-day interactions.

Administrators who attend workshops, seek executive coaching, or publicly share insights from conferences demonstrate that personal and professional growth is valued at every level. Such transparency in their own learning journey underscores that growth mindsets aren't only for students.

From budgeting for professional development to providing planning time for collaborative work, administrators hold the reins on resources that can either enable or stifle growth. Prioritizing teacher development sends a signal that continuous improvement is the norm, not the exception.

A growth-mindset culture thrives where staff feel safe to attempt new teaching methods or pilot innovative programs without fear of punitive measures if results aren't immediate. Administrators who encourage responsible risk-taking nurture a climate of trust and shared responsibility.

Celebrating staff and students who demonstrate resilience, creativity, or steady progress cements growth mindset values. Recognitions—whether through staff newsletters, award assemblies, or personal acknowledgments—reinforce the message that effort and improvement are noticed and appreciated.

Why a Growth Mindset Culture Is Essential Today

Cultivating a culture of continuous growth and learning is no longer just an aspiration but a fundamental necessity in today's dynamic and complex educational environment. Rapid technological changes, shifting workforce demands, and global interconnectedness challenge schools to prepare students for a future that may look drastically different than the present. A growth mindset prepares the entire community—students, teachers, and leaders alike—to flexibly adapt.

Growth mindset philosophies often challenge preconceived notions about student potential. By holding high expectations for all learners, educators disrupt low-expectation traps that disproportionately affect marginalized students. Over time, this can help close achievement gaps, as every child is encouraged to see themselves as capable of growth.

Innovation in Teaching and Learning

Continuous improvement cycles promote creativity and exploration. Teachers unafraid of failure are more willing to try new apps, project-based learning modules, or differentiated assessments. Students, in turn, experience richer, more personalized educational approaches.

Emotional and Social Development

A growth mindset culture integrates well with social-emotional learning (SEL) initiatives. By normalizing mistakes and emphasizing self-reflection, schools create a safer emotional space for students to develop empathy, resilience, and interpersonal skills essential for long-term success.

Paving the Way for Lifelong Learning

Creating a culture centered on continuous growth and learning is essential in a fast-changing educational landscape. By embracing growth mindset principles, students develop a deeper sense of curiosity, resilience, and self-determination. Teachers, supported by reflective practices and collaboration, can refine their craft to meet evolving student needs. Administrators, for their part, shape an environment that prizes experimentation, encourages professional development, and celebrates the incremental progress that leads to transformative outcomes.

Growth mindsets are not a passing trend; they represent a foundational shift in how one perceives human potential. When students, teachers, and leaders collectively accept that abilities can expand through effort, strategic thinking, and perseverance, the door to possibility opens wider. Every missed assignment, every subpar test score, and every tough feedback session become an opportunity rather than a verdict. This reorientation toward growth stands at the heart of meaningful, twenty-first-century education—one that prepares all members of the school community to adapt, innovate, and flourish in the face of constant change.

The Impact of Embracing Growth Mindsets

When growth mindsets permeate a school community, multiple benefits arise:

- Increased Academic Performance of Students: Emphasizing persistent effort and iterative progress leads to higher engagement, greater depth of understanding, and improved outcomes.
- Resilience in the Face of Challenge: Students and staff alike are better equipped to navigate setbacks. Instead of viewing obstacles as insurmountable, they see them as opportunities to pivot strategies.
- Increased Engagement: Learners who feel they can continually improve are less likely to disengage or give up. Their curiosity remains high, fueling a culture of inquiry and innovation.
- Culture of Continuous Improvement: The entire organization—from first-year teachers to experienced administrators—adopts the mindset that growth is an ongoing journey, not a finite destination.
- Effective Teacher Practices: Growth-minded teachers gravitate toward evidence-based practices, feedback loops, and ongoing professional development, thereby enhancing the overall quality of instruction.
- Community Support: As a school demonstrates that it values progress for all stakeholders, families and local communities often rally around these efforts, offering support and partnership opportunities.

Strategies to Embrace Growth Mindsets

Below are actionable methods tailored to different groups in the educational community, illustrating how they can integrate growth mindset principles into daily practices:

For Students

- Goal-Setting Sessions: Help students set specific, achievable goals and reflect regularly on their progress. This fosters self-regulation and a forward-looking attitude.
- Peer Feedback Systems: Encourage students to offer each other constructive feedback, focusing on effort and strategies rather

than personal attributes. Peer review teaches empathy and critical thinking.
- Resilience Workshops: Provide workshops or activities that teach stress management, persistence, and emotional regulation. These skills prepare students to manage academic and personal challenges.
- Celebration of Efforts: Regularly highlight student progress and improvements—whether in small group discussions, assemblies, or newsletters—reinforcing that growth is valued.

For Teachers

- Praise Effort, Not Just Results: Give specific feedback praising the process—strategies, diligence, creativity—that students use. This distinction helps learners see that growth is achievable through focused effort.
- Growth-Focused Feedback: When grading, offer concrete advice on how students can improve, rather than just a letter or number. This transforms assessments into meaningful learning experiences.
- Mistake of the Day: Create a routine where you spotlight a "mistake of the day" (from yourself or a volunteer) to discuss what can be learned. Normalizing mistakes demystifies errors and teaches adaptability.
- Mindset Lessons: Integrate short lessons on brain plasticity or success stories of resilience to reinforce the growth mindset philosophy. Students gain insight into why effort and perseverance pay off.

For Administrators

- Use of Growth Mindset Language: Consistently employ language that emphasizes effort, learning, and improvement in your communications. This reframes challenges as steppingstones rather than obstacles.
- Review and Revision of Policies: Ensure school policies (e.g., grading, promotion criteria, professional development) reflect growth mindset values. This might include encouraging formative assessments or shifting away from purely punitive discipline approaches.
- Encouraging Reflective Practices: Implement regular reflection opportunities for staff, such as monthly debriefs or portfolio reviews, to discuss successes and next steps. Collective reflection cultivates trust and openness.

- Milestone Celebrations: Celebrate milestones—teacher achievements, class-wide improvements, or significant student gains—through public recognition. This highlights progress and reaffirms that everyone's growth matters.

In an ever-changing educational landscape, fostering a growth mindset is essential for continuous learning, resilience, and long-term success. When students see failure as a steppingstone to success, they become more engaged, motivated, and adaptable. Teachers who embrace lifelong learning refine their instructional practices through reflection, collaboration, and professional development. Administrators play a crucial role in cultivating a school culture that encourages risk-taking, values effort, and provides the resources necessary for innovation and continuous improvement. By embedding growth mindset principles into daily practice, schools create an environment where students and staff are empowered to take on challenges, embrace feedback, and persist in the pursuit of excellence.

3 Nurturing Trust and Communication

In education, trust and communication serve as cornerstones of successful relationships among students, parents, educators, and the broader community. Much like a well-constructed bridge, these elements connect diverse stakeholders, ensuring that collaborative efforts, mutual respect, and shared responsibility for student achievement are supported from both ends. Without trust and effective communication, even the best academic programs or strategic plans may falter, ultimately undermining the sense of unity essential for progress.

Why Trust and Communication Matter

Trust provides the psychological safety needed for educators to share resources, brainstorm new methods, and openly discuss challenges. When teachers trust one another, for instance, they're more apt to co-develop lesson plans or observe each other's classrooms, leading to richer professional growth. The same principle holds true for students who, feeling safe among peers and teachers, become more receptive to group work and collaborative projects.

A trusting community helps distribute the responsibility of education across various stakeholders—students, parents, teachers, and administrators. Everyone feels that they have a voice and a stake in the collective mission, from academic success to social-emotional well-being. This shared responsibility can help maintain motivation and ensure a higher degree of accountability.

Sustained trust fortifies a school or district against fluctuations in policy or leadership changes. When new initiatives arise or district priorities shift, a base of strong relationships keeps the community anchored, preventing disruptions or misalignments from spiraling into conflict.

Communication as the Lifeblood of Trust

Communication, often described as the "lifeblood" of relationships, plays a pivotal role in nurturing trust within educational settings. Clear, effective communication acts as a conduit for the exchange of ideas, expectations, and feedback, thereby laying the groundwork for shared understanding and cohesion.

Listening attentively to students, colleagues, and parents is more than a polite gesture; it signals respect and a willingness to learn from one another. By devoting time to truly hear concerns, leaders and educators demonstrate empathy, which deepens the trust others place in them.

Communication channels must be convenient for all parties. For instance, some parents may prefer email updates, while others might rely on phone calls or in-person meetings. Offering multiple avenues for interaction ensures families and staff feel comfortable reaching out, thereby enhancing transparency and reducing the chance of misunderstandings.

Beyond sending out memos or posting bulletins, schools benefit from interactive platforms—town halls, parent-teacher forums, online Q&A sessions—that encourage real dialogue. When communication flows in both directions, administrators and teachers become more responsive to emerging needs, and community members feel their input holds genuine weight.

Educational jargon or policy-heavy language can alienate families and students. Simplifying complex updates into user-friendly language and visuals can significantly improve engagement, making it easier for everyone to grasp important decisions and next steps.

Building Trust Through Consistency and Reliability

Consistency and reliability are two pillars essential to building and maintaining trust. An educator's ability to deliver on promises, meet deadlines, and demonstrate ethical conduct not only boosts their credibility but also provides stability for those who depend on them. Trust grows when teachers and administrators consistently honor their word. Whether it's returning graded work on the promised date or ensuring a scheduled meeting actually takes place, each fulfilled promise sends the message that leaders and educators can be counted on.

Adhering to professional standards and demonstrating honesty reinforces the moral backbone of an educational setting. When ethical breaches occur—such as favoritism or inconsistent disciplinary actions—trust weakens, sometimes irreparably. In times of crisis (e.g., sudden policy changes or community-wide challenges), consistent and transparent leadership becomes especially vital. Families and staff look for calm, clear-headed guidance that assures them the school is organized, caring, and in control.

The Role of Empathy in Fostering Positive Communication

Empathy—the ability to understand and share the feelings of others—is an especially powerful tool in building trust and nurturing positive communication. In educational contexts, empathy bridges generational gaps between students and adults, cultural differences in diverse communities, and varying professional perspectives among staff.

When educators or administrators show genuine care for students' well-being and emotional needs, they transform the learning space into a supportive environment. Students are more likely to confide their challenges, request help, and take positive risks in an empathetic setting. Teachers who feel understood by colleagues and administrators often exhibit higher job satisfaction and are more willing to adopt new methods or share innovative ideas. This sense of empathy in the workplace can reduce burnout and foster collaborative spirit.

Empathy allows educators to see themselves as continuous learners, too. When teachers feel safe expressing doubts or seeking support, they can refine their pedagogy and continually improve outcomes for students. This continuous cycle of growth is sustained by empathetic leaders who validate teacher experiences, both successes and struggles.

Transparency and Honesty: Cornerstones of Trust

Transparency and honesty amplify trust by showing authenticity, accountability, and shared ethical conduct. When administrators and teachers openly share information, admit mistakes, and address conflicts in a timely manner, they pave the way for a positive and enriching environment. Whether it's budget allocations, curriculum changes, or staffing updates, providing consistent and accessible information limits speculation and fosters a sense of inclusivity. This transparency can extend to posting meeting minutes publicly or summarizing decisions after school board sessions.

Mistakes happen in any profession, but owning them transparently is crucial in education, where leaders model behaviors for impressionable learners. By acknowledging errors and outlining how they will be corrected, schools demonstrate a commitment to ethical practices. Addressing conflicts swiftly and with honesty prevents misunderstandings from festering and undermining trust. Openness about the process—who is involved, what steps are being taken—reassures the community that the issue will be resolved fairly.

Enacting Trust and Communication in Practice

Various strategies can be employed to cultivate trust and promote open communication within educational communities. Regular check-ins, whether formal or informal, provide opportunities for stakeholders to connect, share concerns, and celebrate successes. Town hall meetings create an inclusive platform for transparent discussions on important issues. Feedback sessions allow for constructive input from all parties, reinforcing a culture of continuous improvement and mutual respect. Adopting an open-door policy communicates accessibility and approachability, encouraging dialogue and rapport with students, parents, and colleagues alike.

Formal check-ins might include scheduled progress reviews or performance evaluations, while informal ones can be casual conversations in the hallway or quick chats over coffee. Both methods provide valuable windows into day-to-day experiences. There are options for informal tools too. In an era of increased technology use, schools can employ online discussion boards, email newsletters, and messaging apps to streamline communication. However, these tools must be carefully managed to ensure respectful exchanges and avoid information overload.

Trust and communication form the backbone of effective educational communities. By actively nurturing these elements—through clarity, consistency, empathy, and genuine openness—educators and leaders create an environment where students flourish academically and socially, teachers thrive professionally, and administrators lead with integrity and confidence. Furthermore, strong trust and communication practices invite the community at large—families, local businesses, and civic organizations—into a cohesive partnership for student success.

In essence, nurturing trust and communication is not a one-time initiative but an ongoing endeavor. Each day presents opportunities to uphold promises, clarify misunderstandings, welcome new perspectives, and champion honest dialogue. The result is an educational landscape marked by respect, support, and collaboration—qualities that remain indispensable for guiding every learner toward their full potential.

The Impact of Nurturing Trust and Communication

Trust and open communication lead to a shared ethos, where students, teachers, and staff align on the school's core values. A unified culture decreases interpersonal conflicts and supports collaborative planning. Leaders who encourage dialogue and practice consistent transparency earn greater credibility. Their supportive stance further inspires teachers to innovate and students to strive for excellence.

When trust is high, difficult issues can be tackled collectively with minimal defensiveness. Teachers, parents, and students feel comfortable proposing solutions, accelerating the problem-solving process. Students, teachers, and community members who trust one another tend to exercise more initiative. Students might spearhead new clubs, teachers might pilot creative lesson designs, and parents might volunteer more time and resources.

Schools that cultivate trust and effectively communicate are often better supported by local businesses, alumni, nonprofits, and civic organizations.

Partnerships thrive under these conditions, enhancing resources and opportunities for learners. A trusting and communicative environment nurtures not just academic but also emotional growth. Students learn how to handle conflict, practice empathy, and establish respectful boundaries—key life skills beyond graduation.

Strategies to Nurture Trust and Communication

Several practical, group-specific methods can strengthen trust and open communication channels:

For Students

- *Establish Clear Expectations: Communicate behavioral, academic, and interactional expectations so students understand their responsibilities and the structure that underpins their success.*
- Create Safe Spaces: Foster environments—both physical and digital—where students can openly ask questions and share concerns. This might include advisory periods, counseling drop-ins, or online chat forums that teachers moderate.
- Train on Conflict Resolution Skills: Explicitly teach students how to navigate disagreements constructively. Role-playing exercises, peer mediation programs, or workshops on empathy can all build healthier peer interactions.
- Be Consistent: Whether it's addressing dress code, late work, or classroom rules, handle student concerns consistently to avoid perceptions of favoritism or bias.

For Teachers

- Regular Feedback: Provide updates on schoolwide activities, professional development opportunities, and policy changes. Teachers who feel informed can better plan and collaborate.
- Validate Feelings: Acknowledge the experiences and emotions of students, parents, and colleagues—even if you don't always agree. This fosters a supportive environment and reduces tension.

- Follow through on Commitments: If you promise to complete a task or investigate a concern, do so in a timely manner. Reliability is a cornerstone of trust-building.
- Respectful Interactions: Model empathy and clear communication in every interaction, whether with students, fellow teachers, or administrators. This sets the tone for the entire classroom community and encourages respectful behavior among students.

For Administrators

- Open Door Policy: Encourage a genuine open-door policy among administrators, teachers, and staff. Students and parents should feel equally welcomed to share ideas or voice concerns without bureaucratic barriers.
- Explain Rationale: When making decisions or implementing changes—be it a new curriculum or a scheduling shift—offer the reasoning behind them. Transparency in decision-making fosters trust, as stakeholders understand the "why" even if they disagree.
- Admit Mistakes: Publicly acknowledging missteps or oversights demonstrates humility and integrity. This practice underscores that administrators are also continuous learners and fosters a sense of shared humanity.
- Be Transparent: From budgets to hiring processes, transparency reduces gossip and rumors. A well-informed community is less likely to question leadership motives and more inclined to collaborate on solutions.

Trust and communication form the foundation of strong educational communities, fostering collaboration, transparency, and shared responsibility among students, teachers, administrators, and families. When trust is established, educators work more effectively together, students feel safe to engage in learning, and families become active partners in their child's education. Clear, consistent, and empathetic communication strengthens these relationships, ensuring that all stakeholders feel heard and valued. By prioritizing active listening, transparency in decision-making, and reliable follow-through, schools create an environment where trust can flourish. When trust and communication are nurtured, difficult challenges can be addressed collectively, innovative ideas can take root, and the entire community benefits from a culture of openness and mutual respect.

4 Empowering Student Voice

The role of student voice in education has evolved from a peripheral consideration to a central tenet of effective learning environments. In an era where engagement, equity, and personalization are at the forefront of educational reform, empowering student voice has become a critical strategy for fostering ownership, responsibility, and meaningful learning. Schools that actively seek and incorporate student perspectives create a culture of respect, collaboration, and shared decision-making, leading to higher levels of motivation, engagement, and achievement.

Research consistently supports the impact of student voice on school culture and learning outcomes. The Gallup Student Poll (2018) found that students who believe their opinions count at school are significantly more engaged in their learning. Likewise, the University of Washington's Center for Educational Leadership (2015) reported that schools prioritizing student voice see long-term benefits, including improved school climate, lower dropout rates, and increased college readiness. These findings highlight how actively listening to students fosters deeper connections between students and educators, leading to more positive learning experiences.

Empowering student voice is not merely about giving students the opportunity to speak—it is about ensuring that their insights, experiences, and ideas shape the policies, practices, and culture of their schools. When students feel heard and valued, they become more invested in their education, developing critical thinking, leadership, and communication skills that extend beyond the classroom.

Beyond Participation: Co-Constructing Learning

One of the most effective ways to empower student voice is through the co-construction of knowledge, where students actively contribute to the design and delivery of learning experiences. Traditionally, education has been structured around a top-down model in which teachers deliver content, and students passively absorb information. However, research and practice increasingly highlight the benefits of treating students as partners in their education.

The Education Endowment Foundation (2020) found that interventions emphasizing student voice and participation can lead to an additional four months of academic progress in subjects like math and reading. These findings underscore the importance of student involvement in shaping curriculum and instructional strategies.

For instance, rather than assigning a uniform research project, teachers might allow students to propose their own inquiry topics, aligning coursework with personal passions and real-world issues. In science classes, students could collaborate on designing experiments that investigate local environmental concerns rather than following a prescribed lab manual. In history, they might analyze current events alongside historical case studies, drawing connections that deepen their understanding.

This shift in pedagogical practice not only enhances student engagement but also fosters critical skills such as problem-solving, adaptability, and self-direction. When students take an active role in shaping their learning, they develop a sense of ownership, agency, and motivation that fuels deeper intellectual curiosity and resilience.

Student Voice as a Catalyst for Equity and Inclusion

Empowering student voice is also a critical lever for promoting equity and inclusion. Schools serve increasingly diverse populations, and ensuring that all students feel seen, heard, and valued is essential for fostering a positive school climate. A *Journal of Education for Students Placed at Risk* (2003) study found that student voice plays a key role in addressing disparities in educational experiences, particularly among marginalized groups. By actively seeking input from students about curriculum representation, school climate, and disciplinary policies, schools can create a more inclusive and equitable learning environment.

For example, student-led equity councils can provide insights into how school policies impact different groups of students, ensuring that decisions are not made in isolation from those they affect. Schools that actively seek input from students on issues such as representation in curriculum materials, accessibility of resources, and inclusivity in extracurricular activities demonstrate a commitment to social justice and fairness.

Additionally, culturally responsive teaching thrives in environments where student voice is central. When students have opportunities to share their cultural backgrounds and lived experiences, learning becomes more meaningful and authentic. Classroom discussions that incorporate diverse perspectives help break down stereotypes, build empathy, and create a more inclusive learning community.

Authentic Learning Through Student-Led Initiatives

Another way to empower student voice is through authentic, real-world projects that allow students to take leadership roles and make meaningful contributions to their communities. Schools that create opportunities for students to engage in civic action, entrepreneurship, and social impact initiatives cultivate a generation of problem-solvers and changemakers. A report by YouthTruth (2018) found that students who feel their voice is valued are more likely to see themselves as leaders in their communities. Similarly, the Center for Promise (2013) found a strong correlation between student engagement and academic achievement, further reinforcing the idea that students who are empowered to contribute meaningfully to their schools are more likely to succeed.

For example, high school students might work with local government officials to propose solutions for community issues such as environmental sustainability, mental health awareness, or youth homelessness. Middle school students could collaborate with local businesses to develop financial literacy programs for their peers. Elementary students might take part in designing and leading school-wide kindness campaigns that promote positive behavior.

Fostering a Culture of Trust and Respect

For student voice to be truly meaningful, schools must cultivate a culture of trust and respect. This begins with creating safe spaces where students feel comfortable expressing their ideas without fear of judgment or dismissal. Establishing clear norms for respectful dialogue, encouraging diverse viewpoints, and modeling active listening are essential components of this process.

The University of Minnesota's Center for Applied Research and Educational Improvement (2010) found that fostering student voice strengthens teacher-student relationships by promoting mutual respect and understanding. Additionally, a report from the National Education Association (2013) found that students who feel valued in their schools exhibit greater engagement and stronger connections to their learning communities.

Teachers and administrators play a crucial role in reinforcing that student input is not just performative but genuinely valued. If students offer suggestions or raise concerns, leaders must demonstrate a willingness to act on their feedback. Transparency in decision-making—explaining how student input is considered and why certain changes can or cannot be implemented—builds trust and encourages sustained engagement.

Strategies to Empower Student Voice

For Students

- Inclusive Environment: Ensure that all students feel valued and heard, regardless of their background or abilities.
- Classroom Meetings: Hold regular discussions where students can express ideas, raise concerns, and make collective decisions.

- Open Communication: Provide multiple ways for students to share their thoughts, including surveys, suggestion boxes, and digital forums.
- Choice-Based Learning: Offer flexible assignments that allow students to pursue topics of personal interest.

For Teachers

- Integrate Student Feedback: Use student input to shape lessons, assessments, and classroom routines.
- Facilitate Open Discussions: Use strategies like Socratic Seminars and debates to encourage critical thinking and diverse perspectives.
- Incorporate Reflection Opportunities: Use tools such as exit tickets, learning journals, or peer reviews to give students a voice in evaluating their own progress.
- Encourage Collaborative Learning: Promote teamwork through student-led projects and peer mentorship programs.

For Administrators

- Establish Formal Structures for Student Voice: Create student leadership councils or advisory committees that provide input on school policies.
- Ensure Transparency and Accountability: Clearly communicate how student feedback influences decisions and be open about limitations.
- Be Present and Engaged: Attend student meetings, visit classrooms, and actively listen to student concerns.
- Celebrate Student Contributions: Publicly recognize and showcase instances where student voice has led to positive changes in the school community.

Empowering student voice is more than an educational trend—it is a proven strategy for fostering engagement, equity, and lifelong skills. By embedding student voice into daily practices, decision-making, and school culture, educators create learning environments where students not only succeed academically but also develop the confidence and skills to become active participants in their communities and beyond.

5 Community Engagement and Collaboration

To effectively engage the community, it is crucial for schools to understand and implement various models of collaboration that foster meaningful partnerships. Community engagement is not a one-dimensional process; rather, it requires a strategic, inclusive, and reflective approach to ensure that all stakeholders—students, educators, families, local businesses, nonprofit organizations, and government agencies—are empowered to contribute to and benefit from educational initiatives. When done well, community engagement can enrich learning experiences, address systemic inequities, and enhance overall well-being within the broader community.

In the past, community engagement often took the form of one-off events or sporadic volunteer efforts. While these can be beneficial, a more structured and sustained approach can yield deeper and more lasting impact. By seeking collaborative frameworks and emphasizing mutual respect and shared goals, schools can create transformative partnerships rather than transactional ones.

Ensuring that everyone—families, educators, local leaders—knows the "why" behind community engagement helps maintain focus and clarity. This alignment fosters cohesion and reduces the risk of disconnected or competing activities. Rather than viewing community organizations as merely resources for donations or guest speakers, schools can develop lasting relationships that evolve as community needs and educational goals shift. These enduring ties promote consistency, trust, and collective growth.

Collective Impact Framework: A Cross-Sector Model

One model that has gained traction in recent years is the Collective Impact Framework, which underscores the value of cross-sector collaboration and a shared agenda among stakeholders. By bringing together diverse partners—schools, community organizations, businesses, and government agencies—stakeholders can address complex social issues such as educational inequities under a unified vision.

The framework posits that all involved parties define a common set of objectives and metrics. This shared purpose ensures coordinated strategies and reduces duplication of effort. Each partner contributes unique strengths to advance the shared agenda. For instance, a local business might offer internship opportunities, while a community center could provide after-school tutoring. These complementary roles create synergy, enhancing the overall impact.

Collective Impact requires robust data collection and evaluation methods. By tracking outcomes consistently—graduation rates, attendance patterns, or college admissions—partners can gauge the effectiveness of their collaboration and make data-informed adjustments. Regular updates, consistent stakeholder meetings, and transparent progress reports keep everyone engaged and aligned. This continuous exchange of information facilitates trust-building and adaptive learning.

Equity-Centered Community Engagement

While overarching frameworks like Collective Impact provide structure, equity-centered community engagement ensures that historically marginalized or underserved groups are neither overlooked nor sidelined. True engagement demands that schools and community partners actively seek out diverse voices to shape programs and policies.

Conducting community needs assessments or organizing listening circles can surface insights from families who might be wary of traditional school channels. Including these voices early in planning phases leads to more equitable solutions. Schools can formalize inclusive participation by creating committees that reflect the demographic and cultural diversity of the student population. This structural approach helps break down power imbalances and underscores that every family's perspective is valuable.

Holding meetings at varying times, providing childcare, or offering language support makes involvement feasible for families with different schedules and linguistic needs. Ensuring equitable access to participation is a direct way to eliminate barriers. By encouraging staff to deepen their understanding of cultural nuances, schools become more adept at creating policies and curricula that resonate with every learner. Cultural competence in educators and administrators nurtures a more welcoming school environment, thus reinforcing sustained engagement.

Trauma-Informed Approaches to Community Engagement

Another vital element in community engagement is adopting a trauma-informed approach, acknowledging how past experiences—such as violence, natural disasters, or systemic discrimination—can influence individuals' interactions with schools. By designing interventions and supports that are sensitive to trauma, schools can form stronger, more empathetic relationships with community members.

Trauma can manifest in many ways—emotional withdrawal, distrust of authority, or behavioral challenges. Schools mindful of these indicators can avoid misinterpretation or punitive responses, opting instead for supportive strategies that promote healing. Trauma-informed schools strive for physical and emotional safety by training staff to de-escalate conflicts and show compassion. When parents and students feel genuinely safe sharing their stories, they become more willing to engage in collaborative problem-solving.

Partnerships with mental health organizations, social services, and community-based nonprofits can expand the range of supports available. Coordinated referrals and shared data on student well-being can provide wraparound services that address both academic and emotional needs. Engaging trauma-affected community members also means helping them build resilience. This can include offering family workshops on stress management or life skills, encouraging community-building events, and recognizing the strengths and resourcefulness that individuals bring.

Benefits of a Multidimensional Engagement Approach

When schools integrate frameworks like Collective Impact, equity-centered engagement, and trauma-informed practices into their community engagement strategies, the results can be transformative—not just for academic metrics but also for social cohesion and community health. This holistic lens ensures that every stakeholder—especially those historically marginalized—has opportunities to shape programs, voice concerns, and celebrate achievements.

Cross-sector collaborations often unlock additional resources and funding streams. Businesses might donate supplies, nonprofits could offer specialized training, and civic groups may provide mentorship programs. By participating in meaningful ways, families and local leaders develop a sense of ownership over educational outcomes. This increased buy-in can lead to higher volunteerism rates, improved student attendance, and more resilient school-community bonds. Students, in particular, benefit from seeing role models and resources in their schools that reflect their broader community. As a result, they cultivate pride in both their academic institution and their neighborhood.

By adopting a multidimensional approach that integrates Collective Impact, equity-centered engagement, and trauma-informed practices, schools can form more inclusive, responsive, and effective partnerships with their communities. Rather than existing as siloed institutions, they become vibrant hubs where learning, collaboration, and social progress converge. Students develop relevant, real-world skills; teachers gain expanded resources and cultural insights; and families see tangible benefits for their neighborhoods and for the next generation.

Ultimately, community engagement is far more than an ancillary initiative; it is a cornerstone of a dynamic educational experience. It provides relevance, context, and mutual empowerment, positioning all community members—educators, parents, students, and local stakeholders—to work collectively toward a thriving and equitable future.

The Impact of Embracing Community Engagement and Collaboration

Engaging the community grounds learning in real-world contexts. Students see how classroom lessons connect to societal needs, making education more authentic and relevant. Partnerships that encourage problem-solving on community issues—like environmental concerns or local history projects—hone students' analytical abilities and deepen their sense of civic responsibility.

Collaborating with external partners introduces students to diverse communication styles. Negotiating, presenting ideas, and seeking feedback become integral to their educational experience. Students often step into leadership roles when given the chance to work on service learning or community-based research. This experience fosters self-confidence and organizational skills.

When community engagement is woven into the fabric of a school, it becomes more inclusive. Diverse voices and experiences broaden perspectives and lead to more equitable policies. Community engagement can inspire students to take the lead—organizing workshops, forming interest clubs, or spearheading local improvement projects—which further strengthens the bond between school and community.

Strategies to Embrace Community Engagement and Collaboration

For Students

- Internships and Job Shadowing: Collaborate with local businesses to provide real-world exposure, encouraging career exploration and practical skill development.
- Student-Led Conferences: Allow learners to prepare for and lead their own conferences with families, reinforcing accountability and communication skills.
- Guest Speakers and Mentorship: Invite professionals from various fields to offer insight into careers, life paths, or community issues, expanding students' horizons.

- Service Learning: Integrate community service projects into the curriculum, enabling students to apply academic concepts while addressing real-world challenges.

For Teachers

- Cultural Competence: Foster cultural awareness and inclusivity by adapting lesson content to represent diverse perspectives, histories, and experiences.
- Facilitate Connections: Proactively link classroom lessons to community issues or partner with local groups—like nonprofits or cultural centers—for project-based learning.
- Showcase Success: Highlight successful community engagement initiatives, whether through newsletters, social media, or school-wide assemblies. Celebrating achievements sustains momentum.
- Student-Led Discussions: Allow students to guide conversations on community topics, rotating facilitation roles. This practice builds leadership, listening, and collaboration skills.

For Administrators

- Collaborative Events: Organize events that unite students, parents, and community members (clean-up drives, charity runs, cultural festivals), illustrating how education extends beyond classroom walls.
- Social Media and Websites: Use digital platforms to share timely updates, celebrate achievements, and promote upcoming events. Transparency and accessibility bolster community trust.
- Student Advisory Groups: Form councils composed of students from diverse backgrounds to offer feedback on school policies and initiatives, ensuring decisions are student informed.
- Course Offerings: Provide a range of classes that cater to varied interests—from vocational training to advanced STEM tracks—enabling broader segments of the community to engage.

Community engagement and collaboration are not just supplementary to education—they are essential to creating inclusive, student-centered, and future-ready learning environments. When schools actively partner with families, businesses, and organizations, they expand opportunities, enhance resources, and build stronger support systems for students. By fostering reciprocal relationships, prioritizing equity, and embracing a trauma-informed approach, schools create an ecosystem of shared responsibility, where every stakeholder plays a role in student success. True engagement goes beyond transactions; it requires consistent dialogue, trust, and a commitment to co-creating solutions that reflect the needs of both students and the wider community. When schools and communities work together with intentionality and purpose, education transforms from an isolated endeavor into a collective force for progress, equity, and lifelong learning.

6 Creating Inclusive Spaces for All

To build and maximize relationships in education, educators must create inclusive spaces within our schools—environments where every student feels respected, valued, and empowered to learn. An inclusive space does more than meet accessibility standards; it acknowledges the diverse identities, backgrounds, and experiences that shape student perspectives and learning styles. By fostering a culture of belonging and equitable opportunities for all, educators help lay the groundwork for a more just and empathetic society.

Why Inclusivity Matters

Inclusivity goes beyond token acknowledgments of diversity to actively work against discrimination and marginalization. By leveling the playing field, schools become sites where every learner—regardless of race, ethnicity, language, disability, gender identity, or economic background—can thrive academically, socially, and emotionally. When students sense they are respected and seen in their totality, they develop stronger bonds with peers and teachers. This atmosphere of mutual respect and recognition fuels deeper engagement, collaborative learning, and a willingness to support one another.

Inclusive educational settings instill empathy and cultural awareness that stay with learners throughout their lives. Such environments cultivate graduates who understand how to work alongside people from diverse backgrounds—a critical skill in an increasingly interconnected world.

Educators as Key Architects of Inclusivity

Educators play a decisive role in proactively addressing barriers to inclusion. Through culturally inclusive teaching practices and an unwavering commitment to equity, they help ensure that each student's unique strengths are acknowledged, celebrated, and developed. Drawing on students' cultural backgrounds, home languages, and lived experiences can enliven the learning process. For instance, incorporating novels, historical perspectives, or case studies that reflect diverse communities sends the message that all students' identities matter. Inclusive educators recognize that students learn at different paces and benefit from varied instructional approaches. By employing techniques such as small-group activities, individualized feedback, or adaptive technology, teachers can tailor content to meet each learner's needs.

To sustain inclusivity, educators must continuously self-assess and evolve. This can include reading current research on bias, attending workshops on cultural competence, or collaborating with colleagues to share inclusive lesson design. Regular reflection—whether through journaling or peer coaching—helps educators detect unconscious biases and refine their practices accordingly. When teachers and administrators display vulnerability—admitting they, too, are on a learning journey regarding diversity and inclusion—they encourage students to do the same. This openness fosters a growth mindset around equity issues, showing that everyone can learn and improve in creating more welcoming environments.

Emotional and Psychological Safety

While inclusive spaces imply physical accessibility—such as ramps, proper seating, and universal design—ensuring emotional and psychological safety is just as crucial. Teachers can nurture emotional safety by setting classroom norms that promote empathy and understanding. Group activities, consistent routines, and clear guidelines for respectful communication help cultivate a supportive social climate.

Encouraging students to share diverse perspectives and validating their experiences affirm that no one's thoughts are dismissed. Class discussions on current events, cultural celebrations, or social-justice themes become arenas where students learn to listen, question respectfully, and appreciate viewpoints unlike their own. Some students may arrive at school carrying unseen emotional burdens—perhaps from experiences of trauma, discrimination, or economic hardship. Trauma-informed strategies that prioritize well-being, such as check-in circles or trusted staff mentors, help students feel safer and more willing to engage academically.

Intersectionality and the Path to Equity

To appreciate the complexity of students' identities, educators can employ intersectionality: the recognition that a person's experiences are shaped by overlapping social categories such as race, ethnicity, gender, sexuality, disability, and socioeconomic status. This lens helps educators understand that certain students may face multiple, compounding barriers rather than a single form of marginalization. Intersectionality compels schools to go beyond superficial solutions. For instance, a bilingual student with a disability may need tailored supports that address both language learning and physical or cognitive accessibility. By identifying these layered needs, educators reduce gaps that can inhibit a student's full participation.

Intersectional thinking may guide decisions about hiring staff who reflect student demographics, offering translated materials for non-English-speaking families, or modifying discipline policies that disproportionately affect certain groups. By analyzing data on attendance, disciplinary referrals, or test scores, schools can pinpoint trends and address the root causes of inequities. An intersectional approach affirms that students possess multiple identities that shape their viewpoints. In discussions of societal issues or personal experiences, students learn to articulate how factors like culture, family dynamics, and personal interests intersect in their lives. This awareness bolsters empathy and can spur activism or leadership.

Promoting a Sense of Belonging

Another crucial ingredient in creating inclusive spaces is cultivating belonging. Research suggests that students who feel connected to peers, teachers, and the school community are more likely to engage academically, exhibit positive behaviors, and achieve better outcomes. By incorporating group projects, peer-led activities, or mentorship programs, teachers help students form deeper connections. Collaboration also hones social and emotional skills like negotiation, patience, and conflict resolution.

Offering leadership roles—for instance, by establishing a student council that genuinely influences school policies—validates students' perspectives. When learners see their ideas shape the school climate, they develop a greater sense of ownership and loyalty. Hosting multicultural events, highlighting traditions in the curriculum, or forming inclusive clubs—like a Gay-Straight Alliance or cultural affinity groups—bolsters belonging for students who might otherwise feel isolated. Such celebrations reinforce the idea that differences are a source of communal strength, not division.

Acknowledging Privilege, Power, and Social Justice

Achieving inclusivity requires deliberate reflection on privilege, power dynamics, and social justice within educational systems. Educators who critically examine their own biases, positionality, and assumptions about students are better positioned to address inequities. Teachers and administrators can meet in study groups or workshops to discuss scholarly articles, share case studies, or debrief real classroom experiences. Openly discussing how privilege manifests in grading practices, classroom management, or resource distribution fosters a shared commitment to equitable change.

A truly inclusive curriculum avoids a narrow or Eurocentric focus. Reflecting on whose histories and voices are amplified (and whose are omitted) ensures that students from all backgrounds see themselves within the educational tapestry. This critical questioning can lead to broader textual choices, inclusive lesson planning, and even revised course pathways. Beyond individual classroom efforts, systemic improvements—like revising disciplinary codes, rethinking gifted-and-talented criteria, or overhauling special education referral processes—can address structural inequities. By continually challenging oppressive norms, schools move closer to authentic inclusivity.

Commitment to Ongoing Growth

Crafting inclusive spaces is not a singular, completed task. It's an ongoing journey demanding consistent dedication, collaboration, and a willingness to evolve. In an environment shaped by diversity, changes in student demographics, family structures, and societal expectations occur regularly, calling for educators to adapt and refine their approaches. Workshops, conferences, and credentials focusing on equity, culturally responsive pedagogy, or special education can keep staff updated on best practices. Reflection cycles—like teacher-led inquiry groups—help integrate new insights into daily classroom life.

Gathering input from students, families, and the broader community is essential for understanding emerging challenges or gaps. Surveys, community forums, and advisory committees provide channels for constructive dialogue. Ultimately, inclusive values learned at school resonate beyond campus walls. As students grow into adulthood and engage with the world, the empathy and sense of fairness they developed in school can inform workplace behaviors, civic engagement, and cross-cultural relationships.

The Ongoing Journey to Inclusion

Creating inclusive spaces for all is more than a philosophical ideal; it is the practical enactment of fairness, empathy, and shared humanity. By embracing diversity, prioritizing equity, and continually engaging in reflective practice, educators shape learning environments in which every student feels valued and motivated to reach their fullest potential. In doing so, they not only influence academic outcomes but also contribute to the moral and social fabric of their communities.

As schools strive to remain responsive to the evolving needs of learners, inclusivity emerges as a foundational pillar of successful education. Whether through culturally responsive teaching, trauma-informed initiatives, or intersectional data analysis, each layer of attention to inclusion strengthens the educational experience for everyone. By uniting around a vision of a more inclusive society, educators empower students to see themselves as active participants in creating fairer, more compassionate communities.

A positive school climate fosters a culture of respect, empathy, and belonging, supporting both learning and social-emotional well-being. Ensuring equal opportunities allows all students to access the resources and support they need to succeed, helping to reduce disparities in achievement and disciplinary actions. When learners feel engaged and motivated, they develop stronger connections to curricula, peers, and teachers, leading to increased participation and ownership of their education.

Inclusive spaces promote trust and empathy, normalizing compassionate interactions and fostering individuals who can collaborate effectively. In such supportive environments, students also develop better emotional regulation, enabling them to manage stress and conflicts while benefiting their overall mental health. Additionally, exposure to diverse perspectives prepares students to navigate an increasingly interconnected world with cultural sensitivity and open-mindedness.

Strategies to Create Inclusive Spaces for All

For Students

- Peer Education Programs: Enable students to teach one another about diversity, respect, and social inclusion, solidifying their own understanding through active participation.
- Advocacy Projects: Encourage students to identify inclusivity challenges within school or the community, then devise action plans—like awareness campaigns or resource drives—to address them.
- Peer Mediators: Train select students in conflict resolution and empathy skills so they can help de-escalate peer disagreements, reinforcing a peaceful and supportive environment.
- Inclusive Sports Teams and Clubs: Encourage extracurriculars that welcome students of all backgrounds and ability levels, broadening social networks and fostering mutual respect.

For Teachers

- Safe Spaces: Design classrooms and lesson activities where every student feels comfortable expressing themselves—physically, emotionally, and intellectually.

- Multicultural Perspectives: Regularly incorporate readings, discussions, and media that represent a wide array of cultures, helping students see themselves (and others) authentically in the curriculum.
- Restorative Practices: Address behavioral issues through community- and relationship-centered approaches, such as restorative circles, instead of purely punitive measures.
- Inclusive Seating Arrangement: Strategically seat students to promote interaction across different backgrounds or skill levels, nurturing empathy and collaborative problem-solving.

For Administrators

- Leadership Commitment: Communicate a clear vision of inclusivity. Allocate resources, set policies, and measure progress to demonstrate leadership's unwavering stance on equity.
- Data Collection: Regularly track indicators like student participation rates, disciplinary actions, or achievement gaps disaggregated by demographic variables. Analyze trends to inform policy improvements.
- Sharing Stories: Publicize success stories—like improved outcomes or personal achievements stemming from inclusive practices—to inspire and motivate staff and families.
- Action Plans: Develop and update roadmaps for enhancing inclusivity, integrating feedback from teachers, students, and community members. Celebrate milestones and be transparent about ongoing challenges.

Creating inclusive spaces is an ongoing commitment that requires intentionality, reflection, and collaboration. By fostering environments where every student feels valued and respected, schools become places of belonging, growth, and empowerment. True inclusivity extends beyond policies and physical accommodations; it is embedded in the daily interactions, instructional choices, and cultural awareness that shape students' experiences. When educators and administrators actively listen, adapt, and prioritize equity, they help dismantle barriers that have historically excluded or marginalized certain groups. The impact of these efforts reaches beyond academic achievement, influencing students' confidence, relationships, and long-term success. As schools continue to evolve, the pursuit of inclusivity must remain central—ensuring that education is not just accessible but affirming, reflective, and transformative for all learners.

Reflections: HSD2 Student Author Reflections

Aidan Gallegos

As I reflect on the themes of relationships, results, and educational leadership discussed in the earlier chapters, I find a strong connection between these concepts and my personal experiences as a student. The importance of building solid foundations in relationships, as emphasized in the book, resonates deeply with my own journey in education.

As I grew up, I recognized that education does not just revolve around learning but rather revolves around the idea of student-to-student relationships and teacher-to-student relationships. There are an abundant number of ways to define what a relationship really is, although a true relationship is when it has trust and communication, engagement with each other, unbiased honesty, and the ability to grow from each other's feedback. These relationships are what keep students motivated to keep growing strong in the educational system; however, without these relationships, expect many students to have a feeling of aversion. I am writing on behalf of many peers that I observed enjoying the educational system when they have relationships in their lives; in addition, I also observed what no positive relationships do to you in the educational system.

In my school system, we have multiple teachers who have different teaching methods that many peers will find enjoyable and some to dislike. I have seen teachers not even teach before, or when they do, they lack motivation to have that spark in their voice to motivate other students. In another scenario, I have had teachers come up to me and offer their critical feedback, but rather, it helps you stay on track so you will be able to pass. The second scenario helps build the idea of teacher-to-student relationships in the educational system; in addition, having this has brought student passing levels so much higher compared to just giving work without much explanation. Personally, I have had many problems experiencing the first method of teaching, and it has gotten so bad that I had to move schools and go somewhere where I felt well-fitted for my personality—I was not the only student to move.

One thing I also observed is that I see teachers do a phenomenal job when it comes to teaching, but no one is participating except a few students. Those few students have something called student-to-student relationships; they feel that if they participate with one another, nothing bad will happen because they get along with each other. On the other hand, the other students are not participating because they feel a sense of embarrassment or failure if they do speak up; in addition, they may have nobody around that lets them engage in what they think. This is why many school systems lack a lot of student voice, because they feel it is not right to speak up or the authority of the school will turn you down and get you in trouble. For example, when I was about to finish middle school, I experienced this when I had my whole unopened drink snatched from my hand by the vice principal, because supposedly I was playing with it too much—my friends were joking around by stealing it—then I decided to retaliate and say "why." This led me to almost get suspended for asking a simple question, which lowered my confidence significantly.

After that event, I lost a sense of trust and communication with that exact admin. Without trust and communication, I would not have felt comfortable being in a school system with an administrator who just results in suspensions for simple things. Luckily, I was getting ready to go to high school when it happened. This is why relationships with teachers require trust; trust is the building block that allows students to open up about the problems they face and can make the school system a lot better as they grow through student feedback. Also, communication allows the students and the teachers to work together because, without it, no information would be given in the first place. In a situation where a student receives a punishment for anything against school rules, do not take it up against them but rather build with them and communicate what made them do it; it may result in fewer issues in the future about certain school rules. However, school culture may have had an effect on why certain students behave the way they do.

School culture is a significant source of where student-to-student relationships come from, but it does introduce unhealthy relationships. I go to a public high school that many of my peers call ghetto because they dealt with many past experiences with gun violence and fights. One of the many norms that many peers picked up is the right to fight instead of talking it out. I have seen people fight over small things like talking trash without proof or accidentally bumping into each other. About 95 percent of the time, if the people in these situations were by themselves, it would have been defused; however, most of the time, they are with friends, and in order to impress them and not look like cowards, it results in fighting. This is what I called unhealthy student-to-student relationships. If you see your own friend about to get into a fight and you prevent it, that is what gets a better student-to-student relationship because you care about their health and safety.

One thing I noticed about school culture is the lack of creating inclusive spaces for all. School culture allows for certain types of students to fit in; for example, sports; sports is one of the biggest school cultures you can find country wide. However, one type of school culture that lacks a lot is performing arts, although there are many musicians able to join; funding does not allow to get certain materials accessed to run a successful performing arts program. Furthermore, school clubs are also one major thing that can allow for inclusive spaces for all; however, many schools country wide struggle with sourcing the correct funding or leaders to run it; hence, it leaves students without a space to be themselves for who they are. With the idea of creating inclusive spaces for all it helps creates student to student relationships, and that is because it allows for two students with similar likings to bond over something that many others won't find appealing. From a personal experience, I got most of my friends from experience in sports—specifically cross country—being on this team help introduced me to other people who are really passionate about running and helped me have friends that I can talk to about honestly.

There are countless ways to define what a relationship truly is, but a real relationship involves trust, communication, engagement with one another, unbiased honesty, and the ability to grow from each other's feedback. These relationships are what keep students motivated to continue growing within the educational system. Without them, many students might feel alienated and disconnected.

I have observed that students who have strong, positive relationships with their teachers and peers tend to thrive academically and personally. Conversely, I've seen the negative impact when these relationships are lacking. In my school system, I've encountered teachers with varying teaching methods—some that my peers and I found engaging and others that lacked the motivational spark needed to inspire students. The latter often led to disengagement and frustration, driving students like me to seek environments where we felt better understood and supported.

In classrooms where student-to-student relationships are nurtured, participation flourishes because students feel safe and supported. However, when students lack these connections, they often remain silent, fearing embarrassment or failure. I experienced this firsthand when a negative interaction with an administrator eroded my trust in the school system, making me wary of authority figures who seemed more focused on discipline than understanding.

The earlier chapters discuss the significance of empowering student voices and fostering inclusive school cultures. My experiences highlight the importance of these themes in creating a supportive educational environment. Strong relationships, trust, and communication are not just theoretical concepts; they are essential elements that influence the success and well-being of every student. By prioritizing these aspects, we can build educational systems where students feel valued, heard, and motivated to succeed.

Student-to-student relationships and teacher-to-student relationships are a key variable to maintain a healthy educational system. Healthy relationships are defined by having a voice that helps trust be built and offer critical feedback. School culture norms can negatively affect relationships in the school system; for example, it is not cool to be close with a teacher because it calls you a "teacher's pet." Lack of student voice can negatively affect relationships because it refuses the idea of giving feedback when things are not right. At the end of the day, an educational system needs inclusive spaces for all to start relationships that work positively. So, speak up, and tell everyone what feels right.

Part 2
Results

In today's rapidly evolving educational landscape, strategic planning emerges as a cornerstone of excellence, offering a roadmap for schools to navigate challenges and seize opportunities with foresight and precision. At the heart of strategic planning lies the commitment to not just envisioning a future of educational success but methodically working toward it through aligned actions, resources, and initiatives.

In this section, the focus is on the importance of strategic alignment and systems thinking in achieving positive outcomes in education. This exploration examines how aligning goals, objectives, and actions with a clear vision can lead to improved results for students and schools. By taking a holistic view of the education system and understanding how different components interact and impact one another, leaders can better address challenges and leverage opportunities for growth and success.

Strategic alignment involves ensuring that all levels of an educational organization are working toward a common set of goals and objectives. This alignment starts with a clear and compelling vision that guides decision-making and resource allocation. When schools, districts, and administrative bodies are all aligned around the same vision, they can coordinate efforts more effectively and make progress toward shared objectives.

Strategic planning in education transcends the mere formulation of goals; it's about creating a living document that breathes life into the mission and vision of educational institutions. It involves stakeholders at all levels, from school boards to superintendents, teachers, students, and the community, ensuring that the strategic plan is not just a guide but a shared commitment to excellence.

Systems thinking is another critical concept in education that emphasizes understanding the interconnected nature of all elements within the education system. By looking at education as a complex and dynamic system, rather than isolated parts, one can identify root causes of issues and design more effective solutions. Schools are not just individual entities but are part of a larger ecosystem that includes students, teachers, parents, communities, policymakers, and other stakeholders. Considering how these elements interact and influence each other can lead to more informed decisions and strategies.

By adopting systems thinking, educational leaders can better anticipate the outcomes of their decisions, design more effective interventions, and create a more adaptive and resilient educational environment. Systems thinking empowers leaders to identify leverage points where small changes can produce significant impacts, promoting a more strategic allocation of resources and efforts.

Strategic alignment and systems thinking help identify and address disparities and inequities within the education system. By analyzing data and trends across different student populations, regions, and demographics, education leaders can pinpoint areas where resources and support are most needed. This approach can lead to targeted interventions and policies that aim to close achievement gaps and promote equity in education.

Taking a deeper dive into strategic alignment, it is crucial to ensure that all stakeholders within the education system are actively engaged in the alignment process. This means involving teachers, students, parents, community members, and policymakers in the development and execution of strategic goals and plans. When individuals feel a sense of ownership and buy-in toward the overall vision, they are more likely to contribute enthusiastically and work collaboratively toward its realization.

Moreover, strategic alignment also requires ongoing monitoring and evaluation to track progress toward goals and make adjustments as needed. Regular data collection and analysis can help identify areas of strength and opportunities for improvement, allowing for timely interventions and course corrections. By fostering a culture of continuous improvement through strategic alignment, educational organizations can adapt to changing circumstances and remain responsive to the evolving needs of students and communities.

In the realm of systems thinking, it is essential to recognize the interconnectedness of various factors that influence education outcomes. This includes not only academic factors but also social, emotional, and environmental considerations that impact student success. By looking beyond traditional silos and recognizing the complex web of relationships within the education system, educators can identify leverage points for positive change and design interventions that address root causes rather than symptoms.

Furthermore, systems thinking encourages a collaborative and interdisciplinary approach to problem-solving within education. By bringing together diverse perspectives and expertise from across various fields, educators can develop innovative solutions to complex challenges. This cross-pollination of ideas and knowledge can spark creativity and lead to breakthroughs in teaching practices, curriculum design, and organizational management.

In conclusion, strategic alignment and systems thinking are indispensable tools for promoting excellence and equity in education. By aligning goals and actions with a shared vision and embracing a systems perspective, education leaders can foster collaboration, innovation, and continuous improvement within their organizations. By nurturing a culture of strategic alignment and systems thinking, leaders can transform education systems to better serve the diverse needs of all learners and communities.

7 Strategic Alignment and Systems Thinking

In the dynamic and constantly adapting landscape of education, the concepts of strategic alignment and systems thinking play a crucial role in guiding the direction and success of school districts. Strategic alignment involves the intentional harmonization of organizational goals, initiatives, and resources with the overarching mission and vision of the district. It requires a systematic analysis of current practices, a clear understanding of desired outcomes, and a proactive approach to ensuring that all stakeholders are working in concert toward a common purpose.

To achieve strategic alignment, educational leaders must engage in strategic planning processes that involve setting clear and measurable objectives, prioritizing initiatives that support the district's mission, and regularly monitoring progress and adjusting strategies as needed. By aligning all aspects of the organization—from curriculum and instruction to resource allocation and professional development—with the broader mission, school districts can enhance coherence, focus, and impact.

Complementing strategic alignment is the concept of systems thinking, which recognizes the interconnected and interdependent nature of the educational ecosystem. Systems thinking encourages leaders to move beyond linear cause-and-effect relationships and consider the complex web of interactions and influences that shape the educational system. By viewing the district as a dynamic and interconnected system of relationships, feedback loops, and nonlinear dynamics, leaders can gain a deeper understanding of the underlying structures and patterns that drive behavior and outcomes.

For leaders, understanding the complexities of interconnected systems is key to promoting efficiencies, a principle that also underpins the mission for a new company I started with my wife Britney, OptimizED Strategic Solutions. By incorporating AI-supported solutions and automating routine tasks with other advancements in technology, leaders can streamline operational functions—such as communication management, data collection, and feedback mechanisms—freeing valuable time for high-impact educational strategies. These tools enhance the systems-thinking approach by providing real-time insights into performance data, allowing leaders to make informed, responsive adjustments.

Systems thinking is a vital component of strategic planning, offering a lens through which leaders can understand the complex interdependencies within educational ecosystems. This approach encourages leaders to view schools not just as collections of isolated elements, but as cohesive systems where changes in one part can have ripple effects throughout the organization.

Embracing systems thinking allows educational leaders to see the big picture and understand how different components of the system interact and influence each other. It emphasizes the importance of looking beyond individual events or decisions and considering the broader implications on the entire system. By adopting a systems thinking mindset, leaders can identify potential leverage points where small changes can have significant and lasting effects on the system as a whole.

Moreover, systems thinking fosters a more holistic approach to problem-solving by encouraging stakeholders to consider the root causes of issues rather than just the symptoms. This helps mitigate the risk of implementing quick fixes that may address immediate concerns but fail to address underlying systemic issues. By applying systems thinking principles, school districts can develop more effective and sustainable solutions that lead to long-term positive outcomes.

By integrating strategic alignment and systems thinking, school districts can cultivate a more interconnected and adaptive approach to organizational leadership. Leaders who understand the importance of aligning goals with vision and applying systems thinking principles can navigate complexity with agility and foresight, driving positive change and fostering a culture of continuous improvement within their organizations.

Integrating systems thinking into strategic planning involves mapping out the relationships between various components of the educational system—from curriculum development to student support services, staff professional development, and community engagement. This holistic view enables leaders to craft strategies that are aligned with not only their goals but also synergistic, amplifying the impact of each action.

The strategic planning process at Fargo Public Schools (FPS), informed by systems thinking, begins with a thorough analysis of the current educational landscape, identifying strengths, weaknesses, opportunities, and threats. This analysis informs the development of strategic goals that are both ambitious and attainable, with clear metrics for success and a roadmap for achieving these objectives.

A systems thinking approach to strategic planning recognizes the dual responsibility of educational institutions: to foster academic achievement and to enrich the student experience. In Fargo Public Schools, for instance, our Strategic and Operational Plans go beyond traditional measures of student achievement. They include student-experience goals—such as participation in co-curricular and extracurricular activities—as well as operational goals that prioritize timely staffing, ensuring no class remains unfilled for extended periods despite looming labor shortages. These cross-department discussions highlight how adjustments in one area—like incentivizing compensation for critical-need positions—can spark innovative solutions rather than accepting obstacles as insurmountable. This holistic perspective ensures that strategic plans address the comprehensive needs of students, preparing them for success both within and beyond the classroom.

Incorporating this dual focus into strategic planning means setting goals that not only target academic excellence but also promote personal development, social-emotional learning, and civic engagement. It involves creating learning environments that support students' diverse needs and aspirations, ensuring that every student has the opportunity to thrive.

Effective strategic planning requires the active engagement of all stakeholders in the educational community. This engagement ensures that the strategic plan reflects a shared vision for the future and that there is broad support for the plan's goals and strategies. The active engagement of all stakeholders is a crucial component of effective strategic alignment and systems thinking. In

FPS, this means involving teachers, students, parents, community members, and policymakers in creating and implementing strategic goals and plans. When individuals feel a sense of ownership and buy-in, they are more likely to contribute enthusiastically, supporting the shared vision of educational excellence and student-centered growth. This inclusive approach ensures that the plan is grounded in the realities of the community it serves and that it has the buy-in necessary for successful implementation.

The journey of strategic planning in education is ongoing and dynamic, requiring continuous reflection, adaptation, and commitment. By embracing systems thinking, educational leaders can develop strategic plans that are not only effective and efficient but also resilient and responsive to the ever-changing educational landscape.

Recognize that strategic planning, informed by systems thinking, is a powerful tool for transforming educational outcomes. It is through this meticulous and inclusive approach to planning that the system can achieve a future of educational excellence for all students. By integrating systems thinking into strategic alignment, school districts can cultivate a more interconnected and adaptive approach to leadership. Leaders who prioritize these principles can navigate complexity with agility and foresight, ultimately driving positive change and fostering a culture of continuous improvement.

The Impact of Strategic Alignment and Systems Thinking

Aligning resources and efforts around clear strategic goals enhances the overall educational experience and leads to improved student outcomes. By applying systems thinking, schools can streamline processes, reduce redundancies, and operate more efficiently. A strategic and cohesive approach fosters increased collaboration, ensuring that all stakeholders work together toward common objectives in a unified manner. Additionally, understanding the interconnectedness of various elements within the educational system strengthens adaptability and resilience, enabling schools to navigate changes and challenges more effectively.

Strategies for Implementing Strategic Alignment and Systems Thinking

For Students

- Goal Setting Workshops: Conduct workshops to help students set personal academic goals aligned with broader school objectives.
- Feedback Mechanisms: Implement regular feedback sessions where students can voice their experiences and suggestions.
- AI-Supported Professional Development: Offer training sessions on strategic alignment and systems thinking, incorporating AI tools that assist teachers in applying these concepts in the classroom.
- Collaborative Planning: Encourage teachers to engage in collaborative planning sessions to align classroom activities with school-wide goals, enhancing coherence and promoting a unified educational approach.

For Teachers

- Professional Development: Offer training sessions on strategic alignment and systems thinking to help teachers understand and apply these concepts in their teaching.
- Collaborative Planning: Encourage teachers to engage in collaborative planning sessions to align classroom activities with school-wide goals.

For Administrators

- Data-Driven Decision-Making: Use data to inform strategic decisions and track progress toward goals.
- Regular Review Meetings: Schedule regular meetings to review strategic plans and make necessary adjustments.

Strategic alignment and systems thinking are essential for navigating the complexities of modern education. By ensuring that all initiatives, resources, and actions are purposefully aligned with a district's overarching mission and vision, leaders create cohesion, efficiency, and long-term impact. Systems thinking reinforces this approach by encouraging a holistic perspective—one that recognizes the interdependencies within the educational ecosystem and the ripple effects of every decision. When educational leaders integrate these principles into their strategic planning, they move beyond reactive problem-solving and instead cultivate adaptive, forward-thinking solutions that drive continuous improvement. The success of strategic initiatives depends on stakeholder engagement, data-driven decision-making, and a commitment to refining processes over time. By embracing this intentional approach, school districts can foster resilient, high-performing learning environments that not only meet today's challenges but also prepare students, educators, and communities for the future.

8 Governance and School Board's Role

Effective governance is the backbone of successful educational institutions, providing the strategic direction and oversight necessary to achieve educational excellence. The role of school boards, in collaboration with superintendents, is pivotal in this context. They are tasked with balancing academic achievement with the holistic development of students, ensuring that the educational system aligns with the community's values and aspirations.

In the realm of educational governance, the role of the school board holds significant weight in shaping the trajectory and outcomes of a school district. As the governing body tasked with overseeing the strategic direction and management of the district, school boards play a multifaceted and pivotal role in driving the success and effectiveness of the education system.

One of the fundamental responsibilities of a school board is to establish a compelling vision and mission for the district that resonates with the needs and aspirations of the community it serves. By engaging in a collaborative process with stakeholders, including parents, teachers, students, administrators, and community members, school boards can develop a shared vision that reflects the collective values and goals of the district. This shared vision serves as a guiding compass, inspiring and uniting all stakeholders toward a common purpose of enhancing student learning and achievement.

In addition to setting the overarching vision, school boards are entrusted with the critical task of developing and implementing policies that govern various facets of the educational landscape. These policies span a wide range of areas, encompassing curriculum design, assessment practices, student welfare and discipline, teacher recruitment and evaluation, budgeting and resource allocation, and community engagement strategies. I recall a board meeting where teachers passionately voiced concerns about outdated facilities, while community members urged immediate focus on mental health services. Our solution involved a series of stakeholder roundtables that identified the highest-impact facility upgrades—ones that supported both academic rigor and student well-being. By crafting clear, equitable, and student-centered policies, school boards can create a robust framework that supports effective teaching and learning, fosters a culture of inclusivity and diversity, and ensures accountability for delivering high-quality education to every student.

Moreover, school boards are charged with the vital responsibility of exercising financial oversight to ensure the prudent management and utilization of resources within the district. Board members are tasked with approving the district budget, monitoring financial performance, and making strategic decisions to allocate resources in a manner that aligns with the district's educational priorities and goals. By maintaining transparency, fiscal responsibility, and strategic planning in financial matters, school boards can instill confidence in the community regarding the effective stewardship of public funds and the commitment to maximizing educational outcomes for all students.

Beyond their governance and policymaking functions, school boards are called upon to provide educational leadership and advocacy for the district. Board members are tasked with staying abreast of current educational research, best practices, and policy trends to inform decision-making and drive continuous improvement in student outcomes. By advocating for equitable policies, supporting professional development opportunities for educators, and championing innovative approaches to teaching and learning, school boards can cultivate a culture of excellence and collaboration within the district.

In essence, the governance and leadership of the school board are indispensable components of a thriving and equitable educational system. Through their strategic visioning, policy development, financial stewardship, and educational leadership, school boards play a vital role in shaping the educational landscape, fostering student success, and nurturing a culture of lifelong learning and growth within the community. By upholding principles of integrity, transparency, and collaboration, school boards can make a lasting impact on the lives of students, families, and educators, ultimately advancing the quality and accessibility of education for all.

The Imperative of Strategic Alignment

The concept of strategic alignment underscores the importance of ensuring that every decision and policy enacted by the school board advances the district's mission and educational goals. This alignment requires a clear understanding of the district's priorities and a commitment to steering resources, initiatives, and programs in a direction that supports these priorities.

Local School Boards and Tailored Educational Experiences

Local school boards are uniquely positioned to tailor educational experiences to the needs and preferences of their communities. By understanding the local context—including cultural, economic, and social factors—boards can customize curricula, extracurricular activities, and learning environments that resonate with students and families.

For instance, in districts where literacy and numeracy are identified as critical needs, school boards may prioritize investments in reading and math interventions. Conversely, in communities that value a broad educational experience, boards might allocate more resources to arts and music education, showcasing the diverse ways in which educational success can be defined and achieved.

The Pitfall of Single-Metric Evaluation

In today's educational landscape, the reliance on single metrics, such as standardized test scores, for evaluating the success of schools represents a significant oversimplification of educational achievement and effectiveness. This approach, while seemingly straightforward, fails to encapsulate the rich, diverse nature of the educational experience and the multifaceted dimensions of student success. Standardized tests are designed to measure specific academic skills and knowledge at a particular point in time, but they cannot adequately capture the breadth of skills and dispositions students acquire through their education.

Critically, this narrow focus overlooks the importance of developing essential skills such as critical thinking, creativity, adaptability, and emotional intelligence—skills that are increasingly recognized as crucial for success in today's rapidly changing world. Moreover, by prioritizing test scores above all else, schools risk marginalizing subjects and learning experiences that do not neatly align with the tested material, despite their value in fostering a well-rounded, holistic education.

This single-metric approach also undermines the effort to cultivate a more equitable education system. It fails to account for the diverse backgrounds and learning needs of students, potentially reinforcing educational inequities by not recognizing the unique challenges faced by students from underrepresented or disadvantaged communities. Instead, a more nuanced and comprehensive evaluation framework is needed, one that appreciates the complexity of learning and achievement. Such a framework would include multiple forms of assessment, qualitative evaluations, and feedback mechanisms that together provide a fuller picture of a school's impact on its students.

By moving beyond single metrics, educators and policymakers can better identify and leverage the rich, varied strengths within our schools. This shift would not only enhance our understanding of educational quality and effectiveness but also promote a more inclusive, equitable, and holistic approach to student development and school evaluation.

Recognizing Pockets of Excellence and Opportunities for Growth

Effective governance in education transcends mere oversight; it demands a nuanced understanding of each school's unique ecosystem. Recognizing and celebrating the distinct strengths of each school within a district are crucial. This acknowledgment serves as a foundation for nurturing a sense of pride and accomplishment among students, educators, and the community. It highlights the value of diverse educational approaches and successes, whether in academic achievements, innovative teaching methods, extracurricular excellence, or community engagement initiatives.

However, identifying these pockets of excellence is only one aspect of effective governance. Equally important is the identification of areas where schools can improve. This balanced approach ensures that while successes are celebrated, complacency is avoided. By pinpointing specific challenges, districts can design targeted interventions that build on existing successes. This might involve professional development for teachers, resource allocation to support innovative programs, or partnerships with community organizations to enhance student learning opportunities.

Fostering a culture of continuous improvement requires a commitment to ongoing evaluation and reflection. It involves engaging all stakeholders—including students, parents, educators, and community members—in a collaborative process to set ambitious yet achievable goals. This collective effort not only promotes buy-in but also leverages the community's diverse perspectives and expertise to drive meaningful change.

Moreover, this approach encourages a shift from a deficit-based view of education, where the focus is on fixing what's wrong, to a strength-based view that builds on what's working. It recognizes that improvement is not just about addressing weaknesses but also about maximizing and replicating success across the district. Through this balanced and inclusive approach, educational leaders can create environments where excellence is recognized, shared, and scaled, and where every school has the opportunity to grow and thrive.

Preparing Students for the Real World

The ultimate aim of education extends far beyond academic success; it is about preparing students for life beyond the classroom. This preparation involves a comprehensive approach that integrates academic knowledge with practical skills and social-emotional competencies. The modern world presents complexities that require individuals to navigate diverse challenges, adapt to change, and engage with people from varied backgrounds and perspectives.

To equip students for these realities, education systems must prioritize a curriculum that balances traditional academic subjects with real-world applications. This includes project-based learning, where students tackle real-world problems, collaboration exercises that mimic workplace teamwork, and opportunities for students to engage with their communities through service learning. These experiences help students apply academic concepts to real-life situations, fostering a deeper understanding and retention of knowledge.

Social-emotional learning (SEL) plays a pivotal role in preparing students for the complexities of the modern world. SEL focuses on developing self-awareness, self-management, social awareness, relationship skills, and responsible decision-making. By integrating SEL into the curriculum, schools can help students develop empathy, resilience, and communication skills, which are invaluable in both personal and professional contexts.

Furthermore, education systems must also embrace technology and digital literacy, preparing students for a future in which technology plays a central role. However, it's crucial that this is balanced with critical thinking about technology's impact on society, ethical considerations, and the importance of digital wellness.

Preparing students for the real world also means recognizing and valuing diverse learning paths, including vocational training, apprenticeships, and other nontraditional routes. By providing a range of options and supporting students in exploring their interests and talents, schools can help ensure that all students find their path to success, whether that leads to college, a career, or other post-secondary opportunities.

The Complexity of Modern Education

The governance of modern education requires a sophisticated appreciation for the intricate landscape of today's educational environment. School boards, superintendents, and other educational leaders face a daunting task: making informed decisions that support the diverse needs of students while navigating the complexities of educational policy, community expectations, and resource constraints.

This complexity is heightened by the rapid pace of societal and technological change, which continually reshapes the skills and knowledge students need to succeed. Educational leaders must stay abreast of these changes, advocating for curricular updates, technology integration, and professional development that align with evolving demands.

Moreover, the complexity of modern education is evident in the diverse needs of the student population. Students come to school with varying backgrounds, abilities, and challenges. Effective governance requires policies and practices that are inclusive and equitable, ensuring that all students have the opportunity to succeed, regardless of their background or personal circumstances. This involves not only tailored educational approaches but also support services that address the broader needs of students, including mental health services, nutrition programs, and family engagement initiatives.

Navigating this complexity also means engaging with a wide range of stakeholders, including parents, educators, community leaders, and policymakers. Building strong relationships and fostering open dialogue can help educational leaders gather insights, build consensus, and mobilize support for initiatives that advance educational equity and excellence.

Finally, the governance of modern education demands a commitment to systems thinking. This approach recognizes that schools are part of a larger ecosystem, interconnected with families, communities, and societal structures. By adopting a systems thinking perspective, educational leaders can better understand the interdependencies and leverage points within this ecosystem, leading to more effective, sustainable solutions to the challenges facing education today.

In essence, navigating the complexity of modern education requires vision, flexibility, and a deep commitment to serving the diverse needs of all students. It is a task that demands not only intellectual acumen but also a heart dedicated to the principles of equity, inclusion, and lifelong learning.

The True Purpose of Education

The essence of education transcends mere knowledge acquisition; its true purpose is transformative, aiming to cultivate well-rounded individuals who are not only knowledgeable but also morally and socially responsible citizens, poised to contribute positively to society. This transformative goal highlights the profound responsibility of educational governance to prioritize the holistic development of students, emphasizing the importance of nurturing both their academic prowess and personal growth. Education should inspire students to explore and understand the world around them, foster a lifelong love for learning, and equip them with the critical thinking skills necessary to navigate life's challenges.

Moreover, education must instill a sense of ethical responsibility and social awareness, encouraging students to engage with and contribute to their communities in meaningful ways. This encompasses a broad education that includes the arts, humanities, sciences, and physical education, each contributing uniquely to the development of a well-rounded individual. By valuing personal growth alongside academic achievement, educational governance recognizes the importance of emotional intelligence, resilience, empathy, and creativity—qualities that are indispensable for success in today's global society.

The transformative purpose of education also entails preparing students to thrive in a multicultural and interconnected world. This includes fostering an understanding and appreciation of cultural diversity, global issues, and the importance of sustainability. Education should empower students to become agents of change, equipped to address the social, environmental, and ethical challenges of their times.

To achieve this transformative goal, educational policies and practices must be forward-thinking and adaptable, reflecting the evolving needs of students and society. Governance practices must support innovative teaching methodologies, curriculum development that reflects a comprehensive view of education, and the integration of technology in ways that enhance learning and prepare students for the future.

The Role of Educators in Shaping Success

Educators stand at the forefront of realizing the transformative vision of education. They are the architects of the learning experience, bringing the strategic goals of educational governance to life within the walls of the classroom. Their influence extends far beyond the delivery of curriculum content; they shape the minds and hearts of students, guiding them toward a path of continuous growth and discovery.

The role of educators in tailoring instruction to meet the diverse needs of students is paramount. They recognize the unique talents, interests, and challenges of each student, adapting their teaching strategies to foster an inclusive and supportive learning environment. Through differentiated instruction, educators can address varied learning styles, ensuring that each student can access and engage with the curriculum effectively.

Educators also play a crucial role in modeling lifelong learning and critical thinking, inspiring students to pursue knowledge beyond the classroom. They are mentors, guiding students in their personal and academic development, and encouraging them to set and achieve their goals. Their commitment to professional growth ensures that they remain at the cutting edge of pedagogical strategies, technology integration, and content knowledge, further enriching the educational experience for their students.

Furthermore, educators are pivotal in creating a culture of respect, empathy, and collaboration within the classroom. They nurture social-emotional skills that are critical for personal and professional success, such as communication, teamwork, and problem-solving. By fostering a positive and encouraging learning environment, educators help students develop the confidence and skills needed to face the challenges of the future.

The significance of governance in shaping the educational landscape cannot be understated. School boards, superintendents, and other educational leaders play a vital role in setting the direction and tone of education, ensuring that it aligns with the needs and aspirations of students and the community at large. The task of governance is to create a vision for educational excellence that encompasses not only academic achievement but also the holistic development of every student.

Strategic alignment is essential in this endeavor. Governance must ensure that policies, resources, and initiatives are cohesively directed toward achieving the transformative purpose of education. This includes investing in the professional development of educators, fostering innovation in teaching and learning, and ensuring equitable access to high-quality educational opportunities for all students.

Recognizing the complexity of education in today's world, governance must be adaptive, responsive, and inclusive. It should engage with a broad spectrum of stakeholders, including educators, parents, students, and community members, to gather insights and build consensus around shared goals. By valuing diverse perspectives and expertise, governance can develop more effective and sustainable strategies for addressing the multifaceted challenges facing education.

Supporting educators in their mission is a cornerstone of effective governance. By providing educators with the resources, training, and support they need, governance can empower them to excel in their roles, thereby enriching the student learning experience. This includes not only material resources but also fostering a culture of appreciation and respect for the critical work educators do.

In conclusion, strengthening governance is pivotal for nurturing educational excellence. Through strategic alignment, embracing complexity, and supporting educators, governance can pave the way for a future where all students have the opportunity to succeed and thrive. This future is one where education truly transforms lives, equipping individuals with the knowledge, skills, and values they need to contribute positively to society and lead fulfilling lives.

The Impact of Effective Governance

Effective governance begins with a clear vision and mission, ensuring that all efforts are aligned toward common goals. Well-developed policies provide the foundation for both student academic and personal growth while also supporting the professional development of educators. Prudent resource management maximizes the impact on student learning and achievement by allocating funds and support where they are needed most. Additionally, strong community engagement in governance fosters a supportive and inclusive educational environment, strengthening partnerships between schools, families, and stakeholders to enhance overall success.

Strategies for Implementing Effective Governances

For Students

- Student Representation: Include student voice through appropriate opportunities for student perspective on governance issues.

- Leadership Opportunities: Create programs that allow students to participate in decision-making processes at various levels.

For Teachers

- Policy Feedback: Establish channels for teachers to provide feedback on policies and their implementation.
- Professional Growth: Support continuous professional development aligned with strategic goals and governance priorities.

For Administrators

- Transparent Communication: Maintain open lines of communication with all stakeholders regarding governance decisions and their impacts.
- Stakeholder Involvement: Actively involve parents, community members, and staff in the governance process to ensure diverse perspectives are considered.

Effective governance in education requires intentional leadership, strategic alignment, and a commitment to collaboration among school boards, administrators, educators, and the community. When governance is transparent, inclusive, and student-centered, it provides a strong foundation for academic achievement and holistic development. School boards play a critical role in ensuring policies and resources align with the needs of students, fostering an environment where both educators and learners can thrive. Beyond oversight, effective governance embraces a systems-thinking approach that anticipates challenges, adapts to changing educational landscapes, and continuously refines strategies to promote long-term success. By maintaining a clear vision, engaging diverse stakeholders, and prioritizing both equity and innovation, school boards and administrators create sustainable structures that prepare students for lifelong learning and meaningful contributions to society.

9 Operational Planning and Cascading Goals

Strategic planning is a fundamental process that plays a pivotal role in guiding the direction and growth of educational institutions. It serves as a roadmap for setting priorities, making decisions, allocating resources, and ultimately achieving long-term goals. Within the realm of education, effective strategic planning involves a comprehensive and forward-thinking approach that takes into account the unique challenges and opportunities facing schools and districts.

Operational planning in the realm of education serves as the vital link that transforms strategic visions into tangible actions, effectively bridging the gap between ambitious goals and the realities of day-to-day execution. It involves translating the broad objectives outlined by governance and strategic planning into specific, manageable projects and initiatives that can be implemented within the educational environment. This chapter explores the framework of cascading goals, an essential methodology that ensures alignment from the overarching district level down to the nuances of individual classroom activities. By adopting this approach, educational leaders can foster an atmosphere of clarity, achievement, and unified effort across all levels of the educational system, thereby enhancing the overall impact of educational initiatives.

The process of operational planning encompasses the meticulous articulation of action plans, timelines, and resource allocation, all designed to advance the strategic goals of the educational institution. This planning phase is critical for identifying the steps necessary to transition from abstract goals to concrete results, including the development of metrics for success, identification of necessary resources, and the establishment of a coherent timeline for implementation. Through operational planning, educational leaders can ensure that every element of the educational process is aligned with the strategic vision, thereby maximizing the effectiveness and efficiency of educational efforts.

OptimizED Strategic Solutions emphasizes the use of AI-driven solutions for automating routine tasks, allowing educational leaders to focus on high-impact areas such as teaching and learning. In the context of operational planning, AI can assist in streamlining communications, automating data analysis, and managing routine administrative tasks, thus reinforcing a strategic focus on cascading goals. Such efficiencies align with the cascading goals framework by ensuring that leaders have the necessary resources and time to address critical, student-centered initiatives.

Cascading Goals for Clarity and Achievement

The architecture of cascading goals is both elegant and practical, establishing a system where objectives seamlessly flow from the upper echelons of educational governance down to the individual classrooms. This system is not unidirectional; it incorporates an essential upward feedback loop, allowing insights and operational challenges encountered at the ground level to percolate back-up and inform strategic adjustments. This dynamic interplay ensures that the planning process remains both responsive and grounded in the realities of educational delivery.

The crafting of cascading goals serves multiple purposes: it clarifies the role and expectations of each stakeholder in the educational ecosystem, fosters a shared sense of purpose, and enhances alignment across the board. By facilitating a clear line of sight from overarching goals to individual responsibilities, it promotes accountability and a collective drive toward achievement.

In Fargo Public Schools, cascading goals are implemented with input from all levels of the educational community, ensuring that the strategic vision reflects the unique needs and strengths of each school. By fostering collaboration between teachers, students, parents, and administrators, the district is able to create a cohesive framework that translates into real, measurable outcomes.

The Framework of Cascading Goals

The framework of cascading goals is a structured approach that begins with the strategic objectives defined at the highest level of the educational system. These overarching goals then systematically flow downward through every tier of the organization, becoming increasingly specific and actionable. This cascade effect ensures that individuals at all levels, from administrators to frontline educators, have a clear understanding of their role in realizing the strategic vision. It is a process that cultivates alignment, fosters accountability, and engenders a shared sense of purpose throughout the educational community.

Cascading goals are an integral aspect of operational planning within educational institutions. This approach involves aligning individual and team goals with the organization's strategic direction to ensure coherence and synergy across all levels of the organization. Starting with district-wide strategic objectives, goals are cascaded down to each school, department, and employee, creating a unified and cohesive framework for goal setting and achievement.

This methodology is instrumental in ensuring that the strategic objectives are not just lofty ideals but are embedded in the daily activities and decisions at every level of the organization. By establishing clear linkages between high-level goals and individual responsibilities, the cascading goals framework promotes a coherent and focused approach to educational achievement. It allows for the setting of specific, measurable objectives at each level, ensuring that progress can be monitored and adjustments made as necessary. This alignment is crucial for maintaining the momentum toward achieving the strategic vision and for instilling a culture of continuous improvement within the educational institution.

The cascading goals methodology enables educational leaders to monitor progress and track the impact of their strategies at various levels of the organization. By aligning individual and departmental goals with the overarching strategic plan, schools can ensure that everyone is working toward a common purpose and contributing to the organization's success. This alignment fosters a culture of collaboration, accountability, and continuous improvement, driving performance and innovation throughout the institution.

Furthermore, cascading goals provide a systematic and data-driven approach to goal setting and implementation. By setting clear objectives, defining key performance indicators, and assigning responsibilities, schools can track progress, measure success, and make informed decisions to drive continuous improvement. This structured approach enables educational leaders to identify areas of strength and areas for improvement, leading to more focused and effective interventions that support the overall goals of the organization.

Operational planning and cascading goals are essential tools that enable educational institutions to navigate complexity, drive performance, and achieve sustained success. By aligning individual and organizational goals, schools can create a shared vision, foster collaboration, and maximize their impact on student success and learning outcomes. Embracing a systematic and strategic approach to planning and goal-setting empowers schools to adapt to change, innovate in their practices, and ultimately fulfill their mission of providing high-quality education for all students.

Strategic Alignment: Maximizing Impact with Focused Resource Allocation

Strategic alignment through focused resource allocation is a cornerstone of effective operational planning in education. It emphasizes the critical importance of aligning resources—such as funding, time, and human capital—with the educational priorities identified in the strategic plan. Operational planning is the stage at which this alignment takes a practical shape, guiding the distribution of budgets, the organization of schedules, and the assignment of personnel in a manner that directly supports the strategic objectives of the district.

This segment of operational planning is pivotal for maximizing the impact of educational initiatives. By ensuring that all resources are directed toward the areas of greatest strategic importance, educational leaders can enhance the efficiency and effectiveness of their efforts. This focused approach to resource allocation requires a thorough understanding of the strategic goals, a comprehensive analysis of available resources, and a strategic vision for deploying those resources in a way that best supports the desired outcomes. Through careful planning and execution, operational planning ensures that every dollar spent, every hour invested, and every assignment made contribute directly to the advancement of the educational mission.

Ensuring Effective Alignment Through Communication and Accountability

Effective operational planning hinges on clear communication and robust accountability mechanisms. It is imperative that every stakeholder, from top administrators to classroom teachers and support staff, not only understands the goals but also grasps the rationale behind them and recognizes their role in achieving these objectives. Achieving this level of clarity requires transparent communication strategies, regular updates on progress, and a culture that acknowledges and values every contribution to the educational mission.

Communication in operational planning involves more than just disseminating information; it requires an ongoing dialogue where questions can be asked, feedback can be provided, and adjustments can be made in response to new challenges and opportunities. This dynamic communication ensures that the entire educational community is engaged in the process, fostering a sense of ownership and commitment to the collective goals.

Accountability mechanisms are equally important, providing the structure needed to monitor progress, celebrate achievements, and address areas where improvements are needed. These mechanisms can include performance metrics, regular review meetings, and systems for feedback and evaluation. By establishing clear expectations and holding all members of the educational community accountable for their contributions, educational leaders can ensure that operational planning leads to meaningful, tangible progress toward achieving educational excellence.

Operational Plan Completion and Expectations

Operational planning within the educational sphere is akin to setting a navigational course toward a destination, with the strategic vision serving as the destination itself. This phase of planning crystallizes the journey from high-level aspirations to tangible outcomes, acting as a bridge between the ideational and the practical. It underscores the need for a shared understanding among all stakeholders—administrators, educators, support staff, and the wider school community—regarding the goals at hand and the pathways to achieve them.

Operational plans, in essence, function as a blueprint or contract, delineating the specific actions, timelines, and benchmarks essential for realizing strategic objectives. They embody a commitment to a set of prioritized actions, grounded in the collective mission of educational excellence. Addressing challenges such as alignment discrepancies and the necessity for strategic abandonment becomes crucial in this context. Flexibility and a readiness to pivot away from initiatives that diverge from core goals are vital, ensuring that resources are concentrated on efforts that genuinely advance the mission.

Balancing Achievement and Experience: Rethinking Success in Education

Operational planning presents a pivotal opportunity to redefine success in education, advocating for a comprehensive view that encompasses not only academic achievement but also the cultivation of enriching, holistic student experiences. This approach recognizes that education's true value lies not merely in intellectual development but also in fostering personal growth, resilience, and well-being.

By integrating initiatives and programs that prioritize both these aspects, educational leaders can craft an operational plan that nurtures well-rounded individuals. This balanced approach to success necessitates meticulous planning, ensuring that each element of the educational program contributes to a vibrant, supportive learning environment where every student has the opportunity to excel and flourish.

Monitoring and Adjusting Operational Plans

The journey outlined in operational plans is not rigid; it is a fluid, ongoing process that necessitates vigilance, evaluation, and the agility to adapt. Employing key performance indicators (KPIs) and other metrics tailored to the specific objectives allows educational leaders to track progress, assess the efficacy of implemented strategies, and identify areas for improvement. This iterative process is foundational to maintaining alignment with strategic goals, facilitating timely adjustments that keep the educational mission on course even as external conditions and internal priorities evolve.

From Strategic Vision to Operational Reality

Operational planning is the crucible in which the strategic vision of educational leaders is forged into the daily reality of school operations. Through the meticulous application of cascading goals, strategic alignment, and the establishment of clear communication and accountability frameworks, this planning phase transforms aspirations for student success into actionable, lived experiences within the educational community.

This transformative process highlights the importance of a holistic approach to student success, one that values both academic achievement and the broader educational experience. It is through diligent operational planning that educational leaders can ensure that every resource is leveraged to its fullest potential, every effort is aligned with meaningful outcomes, and every student is empowered to reach their full potential. In this way, operational planning is not just about execution; it is about embodying the very essence of educational leadership and making the vision for a better educational future a tangible reality for all.

The impact of operational planning and cascading goals is evident in several key areas, starting with enhanced role clarity, where cascading goals define roles and expectations, fostering a unified sense of purpose across all organizational levels. Increased accountability emerges as strategic and operational goal alignment ensures every team member understands their contribution to district-wide objectives. Optimized resource allocation is achieved through targeted operational planning, allowing educational institutions to maximize resource effectiveness and ensure that every initiative aligns with shared priorities. Administrative efficiency is streamlined by automating routine tasks within the cascading goals framework, enabling leaders to focus more on student-centered goals. Finally, operational planning and cascading goals promote continuous improvement by encouraging regular review and adjustment of plans, fostering a culture of reflection and ongoing development.

Strategies for Operational Planning and Implementing Cascading Goals

For Students

- Personal Development Plans: Encourage students to create personal development plans that align with school goals.
- Engagement in Planning: Involve students in planning school events and activities to develop their organizational and leadership skills.
- Regular Feedback Mechanisms for Students: Conduct consistent feedback sessions where students voice their perspectives, helping educators adjust instruction to align learning experiences with district-wide goals.

For Teachers

- Goal Alignment Workshops: Conduct workshops to help teachers align their classroom goals with school-wide strategic objectives.
- Collaborative Goal Setting: Promote collaborative goal-setting sessions among teaching staff to ensure consistency and alignment.
- AI-Powered Collaborative Planning: Encourage teachers to engage in planning sessions focused on strategic goals and aligned teaching strategies, using AI to streamline administrative tasks, which promotes a cohesive approach to instructional priorities.

For Administrators

- Regular Progress Reviews: Implement regular reviews of operational plans to assess progress and make necessary adjustments.
- Resource Allocation Audits: Conduct audits to ensure resources are being used effectively and aligned with strategic goals.
- Continuous Data Review for Administrators: Holding regular reviews of progress toward cascading goals allows district leaders to make data-informed adjustments, supporting alignment and agility.

Operational planning and cascading goals are essential for transforming educational strategies into actionable initiatives that drive student success and institutional effectiveness. By aligning objectives across all levels—from district leadership to individual classrooms—this structured approach ensures coherence, accountability, and a unified sense of purpose. Effective operational planning fosters clear communication, streamlines resource allocation, and establishes measurable benchmarks for continuous improvement. Schools that embrace this methodology create an adaptive environment where educators, students, and administrators work collaboratively toward common goals. Through ongoing monitoring and strategic adjustments, cascading goals support a culture of reflection and innovation, ensuring that schools remain responsive to evolving educational needs. Ultimately, the integration of operational planning and cascading goals strengthens the foundation of educational leadership, turning visionary aspirations into practical realities that empower students and educators alike.

10 Strategic Staff Alignment

Strategic staff alignment involves structuring an organization to parallel its strategic plan. This approach aligns every function and role within the organization to support the achievement of strategic goals. In Fargo Public Schools (FPS), this alignment is crucial for ensuring that all efforts are focused on achieving the district's strategic objectives. This chapter explores the concept of strategic staff alignment, the importance of organizational structure charts that outline responsibilities relative to strategic outcomes, and the advantages of this approach over traditional organizational charts.

Strategic staff alignment refers to the process of aligning an organization's structure and staff roles directly with its strategic goals. This involves defining clear roles and responsibilities that contribute to the achievement of these goals, ensuring that every team and individual understands their contribution to the broader mission. In FPS, this alignment is achieved through meticulous planning and the creation of organizational structure charts that emphasize strategic outcomes.

Traditional organizational charts typically illustrate a hierarchy of roles and reporting relationships within an organization. While this helps in understanding who reports to whom, it often fails to capture how each role contributes to the strategic goals of the organization. In contrast, strategic organizational structure charts focus on aligning roles and responsibilities with specific strategic outcomes.

Advantages of Strategic Organizational Structure Charts

Strategic organizational structure charts offer numerous advantages by clearly defining roles, enhancing accountability, and aligning efforts with organizational goals, ultimately fostering efficiency and adaptability within the organization. Specific advantages include:

- Clarity in Roles and Responsibilities: These charts clearly define the roles and responsibilities of each team member, aligning them with the strategic goals of the organization. This ensures that every action taken by the staff contributes to achieving the strategic objectives.
- Enhanced Accountability: By linking roles directly to strategic outcomes, these charts enhance accountability among staff members. Each team and individual can see the direct impact of their work on the organization's strategic goals, fostering a sense of responsibility and ownership.
- Improved Communication and Coordination: Strategic organizational structure charts facilitate better communication and coordination within the organization. When roles and responsibilities are clearly defined in relation to strategic goals, it becomes easier for teams to collaborate effectively toward common objectives.
- Focused Resource Allocation: These charts help in the efficient allocation of resources. By understanding which roles are crucial for achieving strategic goals, resources can be directed toward these areas, ensuring that efforts are focused on high-impact activities.
- Agility in Response to Changes: Organizations with strategically aligned structures can respond more swiftly to changes. When the focus is on strategic outcomes, it is easier to adjust roles and responsibilities to address new challenges or opportunities.

Research and Evidence

Research in organizational management supports the benefits of strategic staff alignment. Studies show that organizations with clear alignment between their staff roles and strategic goals are more successful in achieving their objectives. For instance, a study published in the *Harvard Business Review* found that companies with aligned organizational structures were 2.5 times more likely to be top performers in their industry.

Furthermore, research by McKinsey & Company indicates that organizations with well-defined strategic roles see a 20–30 percent increase in overall performance. These findings underscore the importance of aligning staff roles with strategic goals to drive organizational success.

Implementation in Fargo Public Schools

FPS has embraced strategic staff alignment through the creation of organizational structure charts that focus on strategic outcomes. Each role within the district is defined in terms of its contribution to the strategic plan, ensuring that all efforts are aligned with the district's goals. This approach has been integrated into the FPS Systems Thinking and Strategic Alignment framework, which guides the behaviors and expectations for the fulfillment of the strategic plan.

In FPS, the organizational structure is meticulously designed to ensure alignment with the strategic plan. Here is how it works:

- Fargo Board of Education Team: This team, led by the President and Vice President, is responsible for governance, strategic plan development, and monitoring. Their success is measured by the annual monitoring of strategic plan results.
- Cabinet Team: The Cabinet Team, led by the Superintendent, focuses on strategic plan leadership, execution, and results alignment with the district's "Six Rights" and compliance with executive limitations. The district's "Six Rights" are the core systems needed to drive the Fargo Public Schools strategy. It ensures that one's core systems are aligned to make the work earlier and aligned to the "Six Rights" by always asking and ensuring if Fargo Public Schools has:
  - The right people doing the right work.
  - The right structure of roles and responsibilities.
  - The right rewards in compensation and recognition.
  - The right resources of tools, budget, and time.
  - The right decisions being made by the people closest to the work.
  - The right processes aligned to support the strategy.

Ultimately, the success of this team is measured by reasonable progress toward all strategic plan results.

- Strategic Initiative Teams: These teams are responsible for implementing Franklin Covey's 4 Disciplines of Execution team operating system. Their success is measured by reasonable progress toward assigned strategic initiative results, which are monitored through multiple measures. Each team leader oversees specific strategic initiatives that encompass multiple measures from various departments.

- Department Teams: Each department within FPS has specific responsibilities aligned with strategic plan measures. For example, the Director of Standards-Based Instruction oversees the implementation of curriculum standards across the district, ensuring alignment with educational goals.
- Building Leadership Team: Responsible for implementing initiatives at the school level, including staff development and instructional practices that align with district goals.
- Student Services Team: Focuses on measures related to student well-being and support services.
- Communications Team: Ensures that all communication efforts are aligned with the strategic plan, promoting transparency and stakeholder engagement.
- Operations Team: Manages the operational aspects of the district, ensuring that resources are allocated effectively to support strategic goals.
- Human Resources Team: Aligns staff recruitment, retention, and development efforts with the strategic objectives of the district.

By aligning the organizational structure with strategic outcomes, FPS ensures that every role and responsibility contributes to the district's overarching goals. This alignment fosters a unified approach to achieving strategic objectives, enhancing overall organizational performance.

Strategic staff alignment is a powerful approach to achieving organizational goals. By focusing on aligning roles and responsibilities with strategic outcomes, organizations like FPS can enhance accountability, improve coordination, and ensure that resources are used effectively. The shift from traditional organizational charts to strategic organizational structure charts represents a significant step toward achieving greater success and impact.

The impact of strategic plan alignment is evident in several key areas. Enhanced performance arises when aligned organizational structures lead to improved staff effectiveness and student outcomes. Increased accountability follows as clearly defined roles tied to strategic objectives foster a sense of responsibility and ownership. Additionally, better resource management ensures that resources are allocated efficiently, allowing strategic goals to be met. Finally, agility and responsiveness enable organizations to quickly adapt to changes and address new challenges effectively, ensuring sustained progress and continuous improvement.

Strategies for Strategic Staff Alignment

For Students

- Clear Goals: Ensure that students understand how their academic and extracurricular activities align with strategic objectives.
- Engagement Opportunities: Provide opportunities for students to participate in strategic initiatives and understand their role in achieving goals.

For Teachers

- Professional Development: Offer training sessions focused on strategic alignment and the importance of each role in achieving district goals.
- Collaborative Planning: Encourage collaborative planning sessions where teachers can align their classroom activities with the strategic plan.

For Administrators

- Regular Monitoring: Implement regular monitoring and review sessions to track progress toward strategic goals.
- Transparent Communication: Maintain open lines of communication to ensure that all staff members are aware of their responsibilities and how they contribute to the strategic plan.

Strategic staff alignment ensures that every role within an educational institution directly contributes to overarching goals, fostering clarity, accountability, and efficiency. By shifting from traditional hierarchical structures to strategic organizational charts, schools can better connect staff responsibilities with measurable outcomes, improving coordination and resource allocation. This approach enhances collaboration, adaptability, and professional growth while ensuring that decision-making and operational processes align with student-centered priorities. Ultimately, strategic staff alignment creates a unified, purpose-driven culture where every educator and administrator play a meaningful role in advancing the institution's mission and improving student success.

11 Decision-Making, Strategic Decision-Making, and Strategic Execution

Decisions are the backbone of any organization, especially in the educational sector. This chapter delves into the intricacies of decision-making within schools and the critical importance of strategic execution. Effective decision-making in education goes beyond simply choosing between options; it involves considering a myriad of factors that can have a lasting impact on students, teachers, and the overall school community. School leaders are tasked with making decisions that align with the school's mission, vision, and values while simultaneously addressing the diverse needs of all stakeholders.

One key aspect of decision-making in schools is the utilization of data. Data-driven decision-making allows school leaders to analyze trends, identify areas for improvement, and measure the impact of their choices. By collecting and analyzing relevant data, leaders can make informed decisions that are more likely to result in positive outcomes for students.

Stakeholder input is another critical component of effective decision-making in education. Engaging with students, teachers, parents, and community members allows leaders to gain valuable perspectives, insights, and feedback that can inform their decision-making process. By involving stakeholders in the decision-making process, leaders can build trust, collaboration, and support for the decisions being made.

Strategic execution is equally essential in the realm of education. Once decisions are made, it is crucial to translate them into actionable plans that drive meaningful change within the school. This process involves setting clear goals, establishing timelines, allocating resources, and monitoring progress to ensure that the desired outcomes are achieved.

School leaders play a pivotal role in ensuring that decisions are made thoughtfully and executed effectively. By adopting a systematic approach to decision-making, leveraging data and stakeholder input, and prioritizing strategic execution, leaders can lead their schools toward continuous improvement and success. These practices not only benefit the immediate school community but also contribute to the broader goal of providing high-quality education and opportunities for all students.

Furthermore, it is essential for school leaders to consider the ethical implications of their decisions. Ethical decision-making involves weighing the potential consequences of choices on all stakeholders and ensuring that decisions are made with integrity, fairness, and transparency. By integrating ethical considerations into the decision-making process, leaders can uphold the values of their school community and demonstrate a commitment to ethical leadership.

In addition to ethical considerations, leaders must also be mindful of the ever-changing landscape of education. External factors such as policy changes, societal shifts, and technological advancements can impact decision-making within schools. It is imperative for school leaders to stay informed, adapt to new challenges, and anticipate future trends to make decisions that are forward-thinking and responsive to the needs of their students and staff.

Effective decision-making in education requires a blend of strategic thinking, data analysis, stakeholder engagement, ethical considerations, and adaptability to change. By embracing these principles and practices, school leaders can navigate complex decision-making processes with confidence and lead their schools toward continued growth and success.

Introduction to Strategic Decision-Making

Strategic decision-making in education is a nuanced and critical process that involves selecting the most effective courses of action to achieve the institution's overarching goals and objectives. This complex process necessitates a profound understanding of the current educational landscape, coupled with the foresight to anticipate future challenges and opportunities.

It also demands the wisdom to judiciously allocate resources to areas where they will have the most significant impact, ensuring the advancement of the educational mission in both the short and long term.

This chapter delves into the pivotal role of strategic decision-making in the execution of educational initiatives. It underscores the importance of three key elements: alignment, adaptability, and accountability. Alignment ensures that decisions are in sync with the institution's goals and values, adaptability allows for responsive adjustments to changing circumstances, and accountability guarantees that decisions lead to measurable outcomes. Together, these principles form the foundation of a robust strategic decision-making process that drives successful educational outcomes.

Evaluating for Growth: Rethinking Educator Evaluations to Encourage Innovation and Adaptability

Moving beyond traditional, compliance-based evaluations, this segment advocates for a shift toward growth-oriented evaluations. This innovative approach aligns with strategic decision-making by emphasizing policies and practices that cultivate a culture of innovation, adaptability, and continuous improvement among educators. Growth-oriented evaluations focus on fostering professional development and encouraging educators to experiment with new teaching methodologies, thereby enhancing the educational experience for students.

In the context of strategic decision-making, adopting such evaluations exemplifies how leaders can make strategic choices that not only drive performance but also support the professional growth and adaptability of educators. This shift requires a nuanced understanding of the goals of education, recognizing that fostering a dynamic and innovative learning environment is critical to achieving long-term educational success.

Balancing Long-Term Goals with Immediate Needs

One of the most challenging aspects of strategic decision-making in education is finding the right balance between long-term strategic goals and the immediate needs of students and staff. This balance requires leaders to be visionary, anticipating future trends and challenges, while also being pragmatic, addressing current realities and constraints. Making tough choices under these circumstances often involves prioritizing investments and initiatives that will contribute to future success without neglecting urgent needs that impact day-to-day operations and student welfare.

Operational planning is crucial in translating these strategic decisions into actionable plans. It bridges the gap between long-term aspirations and immediate actions, ensuring that daily operations are aligned with the institution's broader objectives. Through careful planning, educational leaders can devise strategies that effectively balance long-term vision with the pressing demands of the present, setting the stage for sustained success and continuous improvement in educational outcomes.

This comprehensive approach to strategic decision-making and operational planning underscores the multifaceted nature of educational leadership. It highlights the importance of a forward-thinking, inclusive, and adaptable leadership style that is capable of navigating the complexities of the educational landscape, ultimately driving the institution toward achieving its mission and vision.

Fostering a Culture of Data-Informed Decision-Making

In the realm of educational leadership, the importance of fostering a culture of data-informed decision-making cannot be overstated. This approach elevates the strategic execution of initiatives by grounding decisions in a robust analysis of data on student performance, program effectiveness, and resource utilization. However, the true power of data-informed decision-making lies not only in quantitative analysis but also in integrating qualitative insights gathered from teachers, students, and the community. This comprehensive approach ensures that decisions reflect a deep understanding of the educational environment, taking into account both measurable outcomes and the nuanced experiences of those within the educational community.

Data-informed decision-making transcends traditional reactive approaches by enabling proactive strategies that anticipate and address challenges before they escalate. It empowers leaders to identify trends, assess the efficacy of programs and interventions, and allocate resources more effectively. Moreover, by incorporating feedback from a broad spectrum of stakeholders, this approach ensures that decisions are responsive to the needs and aspirations of the entire educational community, fostering a more inclusive and supportive learning environment.

To truly embed data-informed decision-making into the fabric of educational leadership, institutions must invest in the development of data literacy among staff and stakeholders. This involves training educators and administrators to interpret and use data meaningfully, as well as ensuring that data collection and analysis tools are accessible and user-friendly. Building a culture where data-driven insights are valued and systematically integrated into planning and decision-making processes is pivotal for enhancing educational outcomes and operational efficiency.

Navigating Change Through Strategic Abandonment

Strategic execution in education often necessitates the practice of strategic abandonment—the intentional discontinuation of activities or initiatives that no longer align with the institution's goals or contribute to its strategic vision. This concept is vital for maintaining a sharp focus on strategic priorities and ensuring that resources are aligned with the most impactful initiatives. Strategic abandonment requires leaders to conduct regular reviews and reassessments of ongoing projects and programs, evaluating their relevance, effectiveness, and alignment with institutional objectives.

Embracing strategic abandonment involves both courage and foresight. Leaders must be willing to make difficult decisions, including discontinuing projects that may have once shown promise or have sentimental value but no longer serve the institution's strategic interests. This process is essential for preventing resource dilution and ensuring that efforts are concentrated on initiatives that are viable, impactful, and aligned with the current and future educational landscape.

The practice of strategic abandonment is not about short-term gains but about long-term strategic health and adaptability. It allows institutions to remain agile, responsive to changes in the educational environment, and continuously aligned with their core mission and values. By regularly evaluating the portfolio of initiatives and making informed decisions about what to continue, modify, or abandon, educational leaders can optimize their impact and resource utilization, setting the stage for sustained success.

Leading with Strategic Intent

At the core of effective educational leadership lies the ability to make strategic decisions and execute them with precision and purpose. This requires a nuanced balance of vision, pragmatism, and adaptability—qualities that empower leaders to navigate their institutions through the complexities of the educational landscape toward achieving success. Fostering a culture of data-informed decision-making, and practicing strategic abandonment are key strategies that leaders can use to ensure their actions are deeply aligned with their strategic goals.

Leading with strategic intent means making every decision count, with a clear eye on both the immediate and long-term implications for the institution and its stakeholders. It involves not just planning for the future but actively shaping it through deliberate, informed choices that reflect a commitment to excellence, equity, and innovation in education. By embracing these principles, leaders can drive meaningful and lasting improvements in educational experiences and outcomes, ensuring that their institutions not only survive but thrive in an educational landscape that is constantly advancing.

This leadership approach underscores the transformative potential of strategic decision-making and execution in education. It challenges leaders to think deeply, act boldly, and lead with a vision that transcends traditional boundaries, paving the way for a future where every student has the opportunity to succeed and flourish.

Strategic decision-making and execution have a significant impact on educational success. Enhanced decision quality results from informed and strategic choices that lead to better educational outcomes and more efficient resource use. Stakeholder confidence grows when transparency and strategic planning foster trust and support within the community. Additionally, proactive problem-solving allows leaders to anticipate and address potential challenges before they become disruptions. Finally, alignment with vision ensures that every decision supports the school's overarching goals, maintaining coherence and focus in pursuit of long-term success.

Strategies for Strategic Decision-Making and Execution

For Students

- Critical Thinking Exercises: Incorporate activities that develop students' critical thinking and decision-making skills.
- Student Committees: Form student committees to involve them in decision-making processes for school initiatives.

For Teachers

- Data-Informed Teaching: Use data to inform teaching practices and decisions in the classroom.
- Professional Judgment: Encourage teachers to apply their professional judgment in decision-making processes while aligning with strategic goals.

For Administrators

- Strategic Planning Sessions: Hold regular strategic planning sessions to review and refine decision-making processes.
- Transparent Processes: Ensure transparency in decision-making by clearly communicating the rationale and expected outcomes of decisions.

Strategic decision-making and execution in education require a balance of vision, data-driven insights, stakeholder engagement, and adaptability to ensure meaningful and lasting improvements. Effective leaders make intentional, informed decisions that align with their institution's long-term goals while remaining responsive to immediate challenges. By fostering a culture of data literacy, ethical decision-making, and strategic adaptability—including the practice of strategic abandonment—leaders can optimize resources and enhance educational outcomes. Ultimately, strategic decision-making is not just about making choices; it is about creating a sustainable framework for continuous growth, innovation, and student success in an ever-evolving educational landscape.

12 Culture of Improvement and Reflection

In the realm of education, the cultivation of a culture centered on improvement and reflection is indispensable for the sustained progress and development of educational institutions. This culture thrives on the continuous evaluation of existing practices, mechanisms, and outcomes to identify areas that warrant refinement and advancement. The bedrock of this culture lies in a steadfast commitment from all stakeholders—administrators, educators, students, and parents—to actively engage in the process of introspection and growth.

To nurture a milieu where improvement through reflective practices is esteemed, it is imperative to encourage open communication channels where constructive feedback is embraced and utilized as a catalyst for growth. This mindset unleashes a spirit of resilience and a dedication to perpetual learning, as challenges are embraced as opportunities for growth and improvement rather than obstacles to be overcome.

Reflection, as a cornerstone of fostering this culture, offers individuals the space to pause, ponder over their actions, decisions, and methodologies, and delve into ways they can enhance and refine their approaches. It is through deliberate and structured reflection that heightened self-awareness, critical thinking, and a sense of shared accountability are engendered within the educational community.

Furthermore, anchoring improvement and reflection in evidence-based practices entails establishing robust systems for data collection and analysis. Harnessing the power of data-driven decision-making empowers educational institutions to align their strategies and practices with their overarching goals and aspirations, ensuring that the journey of improvement is guided by tangible insights and measurable outcomes.

Integration of technology plays a pivotal role in amplifying the efficacy and impact of improvement and reflection initiatives. Leveraging digital tools such as data analytics software, online survey platforms, and collaborative digital interfaces can streamline the process of data collection, analysis, and dissemination, empowering educational leaders to make informed decisions swiftly and effectively.

Driving this culture of improvement necessitates investing in the professional growth and development of educators. Providing ample opportunities for ongoing professional development equips teachers and administrative staff with the requisite skills in self-reflection, data analysis, and continuous improvement strategies, thus fortifying the collective capacity of the workforce to propel positive change and innovation within the educational landscape.

Ultimately, the cultivation of a culture deeply rooted in improvement and reflection within educational institutions is a perpetual endeavor that demands unwavering dedication, cooperation, and a relentless pursuit of excellence. By embracing a mindset of perpetual learning and evolution, schools can engender a dynamic and adaptable environment that empowers all stakeholders to realize their full potential and fulfill their educational aspirations.

Ethos of Continuous Improvement

The ethos of continuous improvement within the educational realm is deeply rooted in the belief that all components of an educational system—encompassing its processes, methodologies, and instructional practices—possess inherent opportunities for perpetual enhancement and refinement. This foundational belief is crucial for cultivating an environment where reflective practices, constructive feedback, and a steadfast commitment to professional and institutional development are interwoven into the core of the educational mission. Such a culture does not merely complement the strategic aspirations of educational institutions; it is instrumental in propelling them toward achieving their objectives, thereby ensuring their agility, adaptability, and responsiveness to the ever-evolving needs of students and the community at large.

This principle of continuous improvement advocates for a paradigm shift in how educational success is perceived and achieved, emphasizing that excellence is a dynamic journey rather than a static achievement. It champions the idea that through a sustained commitment to evaluating and enhancing educational practices, schools can foster a more innovative, inclusive, and effective learning environment. By embedding this culture of introspection and perpetual growth, educational institutions can better align their operational strategies with their overarching goals, thereby ensuring that they remain at the forefront of educational innovation and excellence.

Moreover, the adoption of a continuous improvement mindset encourages a holistic approach to education, where the emphasis extends beyond academic achievement to include the development of social, emotional, and life skills. This approach recognizes the importance of preparing students not just for academic success but for lifelong learning and adaptability in an increasingly complex world. Through this lens, continuous improvement becomes a conduit for educational institutions to enhance their relevance, impact, and contribution to the broader societal good.

The Power of Educator Reflection

Educator reflection is a cornerstone of continuous improvement. Reflection stands at the heart of continuous improvement, serving as a pivotal mechanism through which educators can engage in a deep, introspective examination of their teaching practices, classroom management techniques, and interactions with students. This process of self-reflection is far from a solitary endeavor; it evolves into a rich, collaborative process that is enhanced by the diverse perspectives of colleagues, students, and educational leaders. Such reflective practices encourage educators to view their roles through a lens of inquiry and adaptability, fostering an environment conducive to pedagogical innovation and the continuous enhancement of educational quality.

By committing to regular and thoughtful reflection, educators unlock the potential for significant professional growth and development. This reflective journey is characterized by a proactive stance toward identifying areas for improvement, celebrating successes, and embracing challenges as opportunities for learning and growth. It cultivates a mindset among educators that is attuned to the nuances of effective teaching and the dynamic nature of the learning environment, thereby equipping them with the skills and insights needed to navigate the complexities of education with confidence and creativity.

Emphasizing Continuous Improvement in Teaching Practices

Reflective practice should play a critical role as a catalyst for educators' professional growth and development. By systematically evaluating their teaching strategies, classroom interactions, and the overall impact of their instructional approaches, educators can identify both strengths and areas in need of enhancement. This process of continuous reflection and adaptation is essential for educators to remain responsive to the changing needs of their students and the educational landscape at large.

Valuing reflection as a pathway to excellence entails recognizing the dynamic nature of teaching and learning. It underscores the necessity for educators to be lifelong learners themselves—constantly seeking out new knowledge, experimenting with innovative pedagogical strategies, and adapting to the evolving expectations of their profession. Through this commitment to continuous improvement, educators can sustain their effectiveness, relevance, and passion for teaching, thereby contributing to a vibrant, enriching, and impactful educational experience for all students.

In fostering a culture of continuous improvement, educational institutions affirm their dedication to excellence in teaching and learning. This culture not only supports educators in their professional journey but also ensures that the institution as a whole remains a dynamic, forward-thinking, and responsive entity within the educational ecosystem. By prioritizing reflective practice and continuous growth, schools can effectively navigate the challenges and opportunities of the twenty-first-century educational landscape, ensuring that they provide a high-quality, relevant, and transformative education for every student.

Creating a Supportive Environment for Reflection and Growth

Cultivating a culture of continuous improvement is intrinsically linked to the establishment of a nurturing and supportive ecosystem where educators feel deeply recognized, valued, and empowered to innovate and grow professionally. Leadership plays an indispensable role in sculpting such an environment, not merely by advocating for reflective practices but by embodying them, setting a precedent that encourages a school-wide culture of introspection, learning, and development. This entails providing robust resources, dedicated time, and unwavering support for teachers to engage in profound self-examination and pursue opportunities for professional growth.

To create this supportive environment, educational leaders must prioritize open communication channels, encourage risk-taking in pedagogical strategies, and foster a sense of community among staff. This involves recognizing and celebrating the achievements of educators, facilitating professional development opportunities that are both meaningful and aligned with individual growth aspirations, and ensuring that educators have access to the tools and resources necessary to implement innovative teaching practices. By doing so, leaders not only enhance the professional satisfaction and engagement of educators but also uplift the overall educational environment, making it a breeding ground for excellence and innovation.

Furthermore, cultivating a supportive environment extends beyond logistical support to include emotional and psychological backing. This means creating a space where failure is seen as a steppingstone to success, where educators feel safe to share their experiences, challenges, and successes without fear of judgment. Through such a holistic support system, educational institutions can nurture a thriving culture of continuous improvement, where every educator feels valued and motivated to contribute to the collective mission of educational excellence.

Leveraging Data for Continuous Improvement

In the journey toward cultivating a culture of continuous improvement, data stands as a cornerstone, offering objective insights that can guide decision-making processes and strategic directions. The systematic collection, analysis, and interpretation of data on student performance, program effectiveness, and operational efficiency empower educational institutions to make informed, evidence-based decisions. This data-driven approach not only illuminates areas in need of improvement but also identifies successful practices that can be scaled and replicated.

To effectively leverage data for continuous improvement, institutions must invest in robust data management systems and foster a data-literate culture among educators and administrators. This involves training staff on how to collect, analyze, and interpret data effectively, and how to apply these insights in a way that positively impacts student learning outcomes and operational practices. Moreover, it requires a commitment to transparency and collaborative review of data, ensuring that all stakeholders have a voice in the continuous improvement process.

Utilizing data effectively also means going beyond traditional metrics to include qualitative data sources, such as student feedback, teacher reflections, and community input. This comprehensive approach to data collection and analysis ensures a holistic view of the institution's performance, allowing for nuanced interventions that address both academic and social-emotional needs of the student body.

Encouraging Innovation Through Reflective Practice

A culture of continuous improvement intrinsically fosters an environment ripe for innovation, where educators are inspired to explore cutting-edge instructional strategies, integrate emerging technologies, and adopt novel pedagogical frameworks. Reflective practice is paramount in this context, serving as a critical mechanism through which educators can systematically assess the impact of their innovations, refine their approaches, and share their findings with the broader educational community.

Encouraging innovation through reflective practice involves creating structured opportunities for educators to experiment with new ideas, reflect on their experiences, and collaborate with peers to refine and improve their strategies. This might include the establishment of professional learning communities, innovation incubators, or action research projects, all designed to support educators in their quest for continuous improvement and pedagogical excellence.

Furthermore, to truly embed innovation within the fabric of the institution, leaders must recognize and reward creativity and experimentation. This could take the form of innovation grants, awards for teaching excellence, or platforms for sharing successful practices both within and beyond the institution. By valuing and celebrating innovative efforts, educational institutions can motivate educators to engage in reflective practice and continuous growth, leading to a dynamic, engaging, and effective learning environment.

Cultivating Excellence Through Reflection and Improvement

In sum, the foundation of a culture of continuous improvement within educational institutions is essential for achieving sustained excellence. Through the integration of reflective practice, data-informed decision-making, and an unwavering commitment to innovation and growth, educators can perpetually enhance their teaching practices, leading to significant improvements in student outcomes and the overall educational experience. Leadership plays a pivotal role in this process, not just by advocating for change, but by actively fostering an environment that celebrates reflection, embraces data, and encourages innovation.

By committing to these principles, educational institutions can ensure they not only meet the current needs of their students and communities but are also well-equipped to adapt to future challenges and opportunities. This commitment to continuous improvement, reflective practice, and innovation ensures that educational institutions can maintain their relevance, effectiveness, and dedication to excellence, equity, and lifelong learning, thereby shaping the future of education in profound and lasting ways.

A culture of improvement and reflection has a profound impact on educational success. Enhanced self-awareness emerges as individuals engage in self-reflection, fostering personal growth and a deeper understanding of their roles. Improved teaching practices result from continuous reflection, allowing educators to refine their instructional strategies for greater effectiveness. Additionally, a collaborative environment is cultivated through open communication and teamwork, creating a supportive and innovative educational setting. Ultimately, student achievement benefits from these reflective practices, as ongoing improvement efforts lead to higher engagement and academic success.

Strategies for Implementing a Culture of Improvement and Reflection

For Students

- Reflective Journals: Encourage students to keep journals to reflect on their learning experiences and personal growth.
- Feedback Sessions: Implement regular feedback sessions where students can share their thoughts and suggestions for improvement.

For Teachers

- Professional Learning Communities: Establish professional learning communities where teachers consistently discuss and reflect on the effectiveness of their teaching practices based on whether or not they are achieving their desired student outcomes.
- Action Research Projects: Encourage teachers to engage in action research to identify areas for improvement and test new strategies.

For Administrators

- Data-Driven Decision-Making: Use data to inform decisions and track progress toward improvement goals.
- Regular Professional Development: Offer ongoing professional development opportunities focused on reflective practices and continuous improvement.

A culture of improvement and reflection is essential for fostering growth, adaptability, and excellence in education. By embedding reflective practices, encouraging open communication, and leveraging data for informed decision-making, educational institutions create environments where students, teachers, and administrators are empowered to continuously evolve. This commitment to ongoing self-assessment and strategic refinement enhances teaching effectiveness, strengthens collaboration, and ultimately leads to improved student outcomes. A school culture centered on improvement and reflection ensures that learning remains dynamic, responsive, and forward-thinking, preparing both educators and students for long-term success in an ever-changing educational landscape.

13 Broader Educational Leadership Considerations

Educational leadership transcends the confines of operational efficiency and strategic alignment, venturing into the realm of broader societal and ethical considerations. This chapter embarks on an exploration of how educational leaders can adeptly navigate the intricate landscape of issues such as equity, inclusion, and justice. The responsibility of these leaders extends to ensuring their institutions are not only bastions of high-quality education but also pivotal contributors to the cultivation of a more equitable and inclusive society. This involves a deep commitment to understanding and addressing the systemic inequities that pervade the educational system, fostering an environment where every student, regardless of their background, has the opportunity to thrive.

The challenge for educational leaders today is not merely to administer and implement policies but to envision and enact transformative change that aligns with the ideals of social justice. This requires a nuanced understanding of the complex interplay between education and societal structures, a dedication to dismantling barriers to learning and participation, and a proactive approach to crafting educational experiences that celebrate diversity and promote mutual respect and understanding. By prioritizing these broader considerations, leaders can ensure their institutions serve as engines of social progress, advancing the cause of justice and equality through the power of education.

Balancing Achievement and Experience

In the evolving landscape of education, the imperative to balance academic achievement with enriching life experiences stands as a critical element in molding well-rounded individuals. This balance is not merely beneficial but essential for preparing students to navigate the complexities of a diverse and dynamic world successfully. A holistic approach to education goes beyond the confines of traditional academic disciplines, emphasizing the development of the whole child. This includes nurturing not just intellectual capabilities but also emotional intelligence, social skills, and a sense of global citizenship.

Such an educational paradigm values experiences that contribute to personal growth, ethical development, social responsibility, and a deepened sense of empathy and resilience. It involves integrating experiential learning opportunities, community service, artistic expression, and physical activities alongside rigorous academic curricula. This comprehensive approach ensures students are not only academically proficient but also emotionally and socially adept, capable of empathy, and resilient in the face of challenges.

Educators and leaders play a pivotal role in creating environments that foster these experiences, encouraging students to engage in reflective practices, collaborative projects, and problem-solving that extends beyond the classroom. By doing so, they prepare students for real-world challenges, fostering a generation of individuals who are not only knowledgeable but also emotionally intelligent, empathetic, and committed to making a positive impact on society.

Rethinking Success in Education

The traditional benchmarks of success in education, often quantified by test scores and academic performance, are increasingly recognized as inadequate measures of a student's potential and capabilities. A redefinition of success in education calls for a broader, more inclusive approach that encompasses a variety of outcomes reflecting the comprehensive development of the child. This perspective champions educational practices that foster creativity, empathy, critical thinking, and resilience, acknowledging that these qualities are just as vital as academic knowledge for lifelong success and societal engagement.

By advocating for a curriculum that balances rigorous academic standards with opportunities for creative expression, emotional growth, and social engagement, educators can cultivate a diverse skillset in students. This approach prepares them not only to excel academically but also to navigate life's challenges with grace, to engage with diverse communities respectfully, and to contribute to society in meaningful ways. It encourages students to see themselves as agents of change, equipped with the knowledge, skills, and ethical framework necessary to influence the world positively.

Incorporating project-based learning, service learning, and interdisciplinary studies can provide students with a more rounded education, emphasizing the application of knowledge in real-world settings and fostering a sense of responsibility toward their communities and the environment. This holistic view of success positions students to become not just scholars but compassionate leaders and innovators in an ever-changing global landscape.

Addressing Educational Justice and Belonging

At the heart of contemporary educational leadership is the commitment to educational justice and belonging, ensuring that every student, regardless of their background, abilities, or circumstances, has access to quality education. This commitment requires educational leaders to actively seek out and dismantle systemic barriers that hinder equitable learning opportunities. It involves creating inclusive curricula that reflect the diversity of student experiences, implementing policies that support the needs of all learners, and fostering an environment where diversity is celebrated, and every student feels that they belong.

Efforts to promote educational justice and belonging extend beyond addressing overt discrimination. They involve examining and revising institutional policies, teaching practices, and curricular materials to ensure they do not inadvertently perpetuate biases or inequalities. Leaders must also invest in professional development for staff on cultural competency, anti-racist teaching practices, and inclusive pedagogies to ensure educators are equipped to support a diverse student body.

By prioritizing equity and inclusion, educational institutions can become catalysts for social change, preparing students to thrive in and contribute to a multicultural world. This involves not only adapting teaching methods and materials to be more inclusive but also actively working to create spaces where all students can see themselves represented and feel a sense of belonging.

Learning from Healthcare to Measure What Matters

Drawing parallels between education and healthcare, this segment emphasizes the importance of adopting metrics that truly reflect the well-being and success of students. Just as healthcare has evolved to focus on holistic patient outcomes rather than solely on treatment interventions, education must shift toward evaluating student success through a more comprehensive lens. This entails measuring academic achievements alongside social-emotional well-being, engagement, and personal development.

Adopting student-centered metrics requires a nuanced understanding of what success looks like for each learner, recognizing that achievement is multifaceted and deeply personal. It involves collecting and analyzing data on various aspects of student life and learning, including emotional well-being, social skills, engagement with learning, and resilience in the face of adversity. By focusing on these broader measures, educational leaders can identify gaps in support, tailor interventions more effectively, and create an educational environment that nurtures every aspect of student development.

This comprehensive approach to measuring success underscores the need for educational systems to adapt and innovate, ensuring that they not only meet academic standards but also support the holistic development of students. By learning from healthcare's focus on holistic outcomes, educational leaders can foster environments that prioritize the well-being and holistic success of all students, laying the foundation for a more equitable, inclusive, and compassionate society.

Advocating for LGBTQIA2S+ Rights and Disability Justice

In modern society, the unequivocal advocacy for the rights and inclusion of all students, particularly those from LGBTQIA2S+ communities and individuals with disabilities, stands as a cornerstone of progressive educational leadership. This advocacy transcends the mere creation of supportive policies; it requires the fostering of a school culture steeped in the principles of diversity, equity, and unconditional respect. Educational leaders must champion initiatives that ensure every student, irrespective of their sexual orientation, gender identity, or physical and mental abilities, feels seen, valued, and embraced within the school community.

To genuinely advocate for LGBTQIA2S+ rights and disability justice, educational institutions must undertake comprehensive efforts to educate their communities about the importance of diversity and the adverse impacts of discrimination and exclusion. This includes integrating LGBTQIA2S+ and disability studies into the curriculum, providing professional development for staff on inclusive practices, and establishing clear protocols for addressing instances of discrimination. Furthermore, creating student-led groups and forums that give voice to LGBTQIA2S+ students and students with disabilities can significantly enhance their visibility and promote a culture of inclusivity and respect.

Moreover, ensuring that all school facilities are accessible, and all educational materials are available in formats that are inclusive of diverse learning needs reflects a tangible commitment to disability justice. By actively removing physical, social, and academic barriers, educational leaders can create an environment where all students have the opportunity to succeed and feel a sense of belonging.

Implementing Restorative Practices

The shift toward restorative practices within educational settings marks a significant departure from traditional disciplinary approaches, paving the way for a more empathetic, constructive, and healing-oriented approach to conflict resolution and community building. This paradigm emphasizes the importance of dialogue, mutual understanding, and the restoration of relationships over punitive measures that often exacerbate feelings of alienation and resentment.

Implementing restorative practices requires a foundational change in the ethos of educational institutions, necessitating training for educators and staff in restorative techniques and the creation of structured opportunities for students to engage in restorative circles and dialogues. Such practices encourage accountability, foster a deep sense of community, and promote a culture of empathy and mutual respect among students and staff alike.

Restorative practices also extend to how schools engage with parents and the wider community, emphasizing collaboration and partnership in supporting the emotional and social development of students. By adopting restorative approaches, schools not only improve their disciplinary outcomes but also contribute to the holistic well-being of their students, creating a more cohesive, supportive, and positive learning environment.

Navigating Strategic Abandonment and Change Management

Effective educational leadership in today's rapidly evolving landscape is marked by the capacity to navigate change with foresight, agility, and compassion. This includes the strategic abandonment of practices and initiatives that no longer align with the institution's mission or the current educational climate. Successful change management involves a proactive approach to identifying areas in need of improvement or evolution and engaging all stakeholders in the transition process through transparent communication, empathy, and comprehensive support.

The process of navigating change also requires a commitment to continuous learning and adaptation, encouraging feedback from students, staff, and the community to inform decision-making and ensure that changes are responsive to the needs of the school community. Effective leaders foster a culture of innovation and resilience, preparing their institutions to respond to challenges and opportunities with creativity and confidence.

Moreover, change management within educational settings demands a nuanced understanding of the emotional and psychological impacts of change on individuals and communities. Leaders must provide resources and support systems to help students and staff navigate these transitions, ensuring that the process of change strengthens rather than undermines the institution's core values and objectives.

Leading Internally and Externally

In addition to the foundational principles and considerations previously outlined, educational leaders must also grapple with the complex interplay of external factors that shape the educational landscape. From policy changes and regulatory frameworks to demographic shifts and economic trends, leaders must adeptly navigate a myriad of external forces that impact their institutions.

Policy changes at the local, state, and national levels play a significant role in shaping the educational context in which leaders operate. Educational leaders must stay informed about policy developments, legislative mandates, and regulatory requirements that influence school operations, funding mechanisms, curriculum standards, and accountability measures. By understanding and responding to policy changes, leaders can ensure that their institutions remain compliant and aligned with prevailing educational priorities and initiatives.

Demographic shifts and changing student populations present another important consideration for educational leaders. As communities evolve and diversify, leaders must be attuned to the unique needs, backgrounds, and experiences of their students. Culturally responsive leadership practices can help leaders create inclusive and welcoming environments that honor the diversity of their student body and foster a sense of belonging for all learners. By valuing and leveraging the rich tapestry of cultural backgrounds within their schools, leaders can promote educational justice, foster positive relationships, and enhance student engagement and achievement.

Economic trends and budget constraints also pose challenges for educational leaders seeking to optimize resources and provide high-quality educational experiences for their students. Leaders must engage in strategic financial planning, resource allocation, and budget management to ensure that limited resources are allocated effectively and efficiently to support student learning and institutional priorities. By prioritizing fiscal transparency, accountability, and sustainability, leaders can make informed decisions that maximize the impact of available resources and promote long-term financial health and stability for their institutions.

Furthermore, technological advancements and digital transformation are reshaping the way education is delivered and experienced. Educational leaders must embrace innovation, leverage technology tools and platforms, and cultivate digital literacy competencies among students and staff to enhance teaching and learning outcomes. By integrating technology thoughtfully and intentionally into the educational process, leaders can expand access to learning opportunities, promote personalized instruction, and prepare students for success in a rapidly evolving digital world.

In summary, educational leadership is a multifaceted and dynamic endeavor that requires leaders to navigate a complex web of internal and external factors. By staying informed about policy changes, embracing diversity and inclusivity, managing resources effectively, and harnessing the power of technology, educational leaders can position their institutions for success and create impactful learning experiences that empower all students to thrive academically, socially, and emotionally.

The horizon of educational leadership is vast and demands a vision that transcends traditional academic metrics, embracing a profound commitment to social justice, equity, and inclusion. By integrating the diverse considerations outlined throughout this chapter, educational leaders have the opportunity to redefine their institutions as engines of societal transformation. This vision of leadership is not content with mere academic excellence; it strives to cultivate an educational environment where every student is empowered to become a thoughtful, compassionate, and active participant in creating a more just, equitable, and inclusive world.

Leadership for a better educational future is characterized by an unwavering dedication to uplifting every student's voice, dismantling systemic barriers to success, and fostering a community where diversity is celebrated, and every individual can thrive. Through such leadership, educational institutions can become beacons of hope and catalysts for change, inspiring students to carry forward the values of equity and inclusion into the broader society.

Broader educational leadership considerations have a significant impact on the overall effectiveness of schools and districts. Equity and inclusion are strengthened by addressing systemic barriers and fostering diversity, creating a more inclusive learning environment. Holistic development ensures that education supports the whole child, emphasizing social, emotional, and academic growth. Community engagement plays a crucial role in strengthening relationships and encouraging collaboration, leading to a more supportive and invested educational community. Finally, adaptive leadership equips leaders to navigate the complexities of the educational landscape, enabling institutions to remain responsive to evolving challenges and opportunities.

Strategies for Broader Educational Leadership Considerations

For Students

- Inclusive Programs: Develop programs that celebrate diversity and promote inclusivity, ensuring all students feel valued and supported.
- Community Service Projects: Engage students in community service projects to foster a sense of social responsibility and connection.

For Teachers

- Cultural Competency Training: Provide training on cultural competency and inclusive teaching practices to better support diverse student populations.
- Collaborative Planning: Encourage teachers to collaborate on developing and implementing inclusive curricula and teaching strategies.

For Administrators

- Policy Review and Development: Regularly review and update policies to ensure they promote equity and inclusion.
- Stakeholder Involvement: Involve a diverse range of stakeholders in decision-making processes to ensure multiple perspectives are considered.

Broader educational leadership considerations extend beyond traditional academic priorities to encompass equity, inclusion, community engagement, and systemic change. Effective leaders recognize that schools are not just places of learning but also powerful agents of social transformation. By fostering an inclusive culture, addressing systemic barriers, and ensuring every student has access to opportunities for success, leaders can create institutions that prepare students for both academic and civic life. This requires a commitment to adaptive leadership, collaboration with diverse stakeholders, and a willingness to challenge outdated practices in favor of progressive, student-centered approaches. By embracing these broader considerations, educational leaders can ensure that their schools are places where all students feel valued, supported, and empowered to thrive in an evolving world.

Reflections: FPS Student Author

Zahabu Christine

Where do I start? My journey began when I was just 2 1/2 years old, making the move from Uganda to Fargo, North Dakota. Early memories include starting preschool in the Fargo North area and later attending Ledon Kindergarten Center.

Transitioning to West Fargo schools for elementary education felt like a natural step, finding familiarity and a supportive community. Despite cultural adjustments, I thrived academically and discovered a passion for reading and art, sparking my curiosity and creativity. Throughout elementary school, I built lasting friendships and learned important lessons about resilience and adaptability. These experiences not only laid the foundation for my education but also shaped my sense of identity and belonging in a new environment.

Moving to a new district in the eighth grade was a significant change for me. Up until then, middle school had been a mix of familiar faces and the challenges of growing up. As a girl, I navigated through drama, puberty, and the evolving dynamics of friendships. Despite these complexities, I felt comfortable in my school environment. When I first heard about the move, I was actually excited. I had heard positive things about the new district and knew I had a friend there, which eased some of my initial worries. However, as the reality set in, leaving behind the people and routines I had grown attached to become more difficult.

Even though the new district was just fifteen minutes away, the emotional impact was significant. Adjusting to a different environment, making new friends, and adapting to new teachers and routines challenged me in unexpected ways. The familiar faces and comfort of my old school were suddenly replaced by uncertainty and the need to navigate a new social landscape.

Reflecting on this experience, I realize how much I grew during that time. Moving forced me to adapt, be open to change, and step out of my comfort zone. While it was challenging, it also presented opportunities to learn and develop resiliency. Ultimately, it was a pivotal experience that shaped my understanding of friendships, change, and the importance of embracing new experiences.

Upon arriving at the new school, things took a turn for the worse. I encountered racism and name-calling, which I wasn't prepared for. The school was more predominantly white than my previous one, and I struggled to make friends and adapt to the new environment and education system. While my old district used an advanced-based grading system with numbers 1–4, this school followed the traditional ABCD grading system, which was easier for me to understand but still required adjustment.

Just as I was beginning to find my footing, the Covid-19 pandemic struck, turning everything upside down. Classes moved online, and I had to isolate myself due to quarantine. Transitioning to online learning was particularly challenging for me, as I thrived in smaller, in-person groups where I could interact directly with teachers and peers. The shift to a virtual classroom required me to develop new skills in self-discipline and time management.

The pandemic added another layer of difficulty to an already tough year. I felt disconnected and struggled to stay engaged with my studies while navigating the new online format. Social isolation compounded these challenges, making it hard to find support and maintain motivation.

Now let's get into the good stuff. My freshman year started with a hybrid schedule: online classes one day and in-person classes the next. This routine quickly became exhausting. The in-person classes weren't too bad, but the masks and social distancing made it hard to connect with others and make friends. The constant switch between online and physical classrooms added to the difficulty.

Despite these challenges, I worked hard to adjust. I hoped things would get easier, but the situation only seemed to get more complicated. I fell into some bad habits. It was a frustrating time, but it was also a period of important lessons and growth.

Freshman year taught me a lot about resilience and self-improvement. I learned that dealing with challenges is a part of life and that overcoming them takes patience and effort. Although the year was tough, it set the stage for personal growth and taught me valuable lessons about adapting to change and improving myself.

Sophomore year was a turning point. We had more opportunities to see people and interact, which was a welcome change. I thrived in my classes, staying engaged even when we had to switch to online learning occasionally. This year was about self-discovery—I enjoyed experimenting with new activities, changing my hairstyle, and making new friends. Most importantly, I learned to advocate for myself, a skill that proved invaluable. Despite some drama, I built lasting friendships and gained important insights from these experiences.

Junior year, however, was horrific. I started the school year with high hopes, only to be overwhelmed by a particularly challenging class. Despite my best efforts and utilizing all available resources, the situation became increasingly difficult. For months, I pleaded with counselors and teachers for help, but my concerns were largely ignored. Eventually, I had to complete the class during my senior year. This period was marked by isolation and struggle; I distanced myself from others and, at times, felt like giving up.

However, an unexpected opportunity emerged: I joined the superintendent's student lunches. These meetings became a highlight of my junior year. They gave me a platform to voice necessary changes, advocate for minorities, and represent the student body of Fargo North. This role provided a sense of purpose and belonging, helping me to regain confidence despite the difficulties of the year.

Being part of the superintendent's student luncheons not only offered a sense of community but also taught me the value of advocacy and perseverance. It was an experience that shaped my leadership skills and reinforced my ability to make a difference. As I approached senior year, I carried forward these lessons, determined to navigate challenges with resilience and contribute positively to my school community.

Around September 2022, I started Algebra II. Initially, the class seemed manageable, but soon I sensed something was wrong. I began to struggle, which was unusual for me. Despite my best efforts, my teacher told me I would fail. It was discouraging, but I continued to push myself. Eventually, someone listened and took action. I switched to an online class for the rest of the semester and then moved back to an in-person class the next semester. Starting the online class just a month or two before the semester ended made things even tougher. I ended up finishing that online class during my senior year, which wasn't bad but was definitely challenging.

Transitioning to the online class was daunting. I had to catch up on missed material quickly and adapt to a new learning environment. The online platform required self-discipline and time management skills that I had to develop quickly. Balancing my coursework with my other classes became a daily struggle. Despite the challenges, there were positive aspects. The flexibility of the online class allowed me to work at my own pace, which was a relief from the pressure of the traditional classroom setting. This independence in learning was empowering, although it came with its own set of challenges and responsibilities.

Going back to an in-person class the following semester brought its own adjustments. I had become accustomed to the solitary nature of online learning, so being back in a classroom with peers and a teacher was initially overwhelming. However, I soon realized the value of face-to-face interaction for asking questions and getting immediate feedback. Building relationships with classmates and participating in group activities helped me regain confidence.

Senior year—it's finally here. This year has been nothing short of remarkable. Even though I faced challenges with some classes, I persevered and made it through. I forged incredible friendships and created memories that will last a lifetime. Throughout my school years, I have learned so much, and my mind continues to grow with every new lesson. I'll never forget the people who stood by me, whether they are still with me or not. They taught me, supported me, and helped shape who I am today. Life has a way of taking you to unexpected places, and all you can do is be grateful for the journey.

Public schooling has truly been a lifesaver for me. Coming from a background where early education wasn't always available and where completing school was a challenge, being a first-generation college student or graduate is an incredible achievement. These accomplishments make those back home proud, my family proud, and even those who may not know me proud. Life is full of challenges, but you push through.

West Fargo Public Schools and Fargo Public Schools have given me the education and experiences I needed to succeed. The moments that made me who I am today are unforgettable. Several key moments during my senior year stand out. There was a time when I wasn't sure if I wanted to go to college. The support from my teachers and mentors during this period was invaluable. They stood by me, helping me navigate my doubts and fears. The encouragement from my parents and family made all the difference. I am grateful to God for what I have, what I am going to have, and what I will achieve in the future. Every day is a new learning opportunity.

Before graduation, I had the honor of making a speech. I didn't craft that speech alone; I had help. My father's encouragement made it a memorable moment. I made him especially proud. His kindness, loving heart, and support motivated me to achieve something incredible.

My K-12 experience, including preschool, took me a long way. Going to school for most of your life and continuing right after you graduate is an experience in itself. Moving to different schools had the most impact on me. Making friends, learning new things, and creating bonds and relationships with teachers are what you look forward to when you go to school, even if you don't want to. School was hard, but if I had the chance to go back, I would, just in my own way.

The discussions on strategic alignment, governance, and systems thinking in the preceding chapters have given me a deeper understanding of how these concepts impact my educational experience. Reflecting on these ideas, I see how they play a crucial role in shaping the effectiveness and inclusivity of our school systems.

As a student, I've often felt the effects of strategic decisions made at higher levels of the school system, sometimes without a clear understanding of their purpose or impact on my daily life. However, when schools implement strategic alignment effectively—ensuring that every action, resource, and decision is connected to a broader educational vision—the benefits are palpable. Students like me experience a more cohesive, supportive, and goal-oriented learning environment.

Governance and the role of school boards, as discussed in the book, also resonate with my experiences. I have seen how decisions made by those in leadership positions can either uplift or hinder students' progress. When these leaders engage with students, listen to our needs, and make informed decisions based on our realities, the entire educational system becomes more responsive and effective.

Finally, the importance of operational planning and cascading goals, as outlined in the book, cannot be overstated. Even as a student, I recognize the need for clear communication and alignment across all levels of the school system. When everyone—from administrators to teachers to students—is working toward the same objectives, the educational experience is richer and more fulfilling.

The themes of strategic alignment and governance discussed in the earlier chapters are not abstract ideas; they directly affect how students like me experience education. By focusing on clear goals, effective communication, and responsive governance, we can create a school system that truly meets the needs of all students, ensuring that every one of us has the opportunity to succeed and thrive.

For all you readers, be grateful for what you have and try your best to finish school. Life will take you somewhere, and you just have to hope and wait for it. Hope and faith are all you need at the lowest times. As I look back on my journey—from Uganda to Fargo—every challenge became an opportunity for growth. The district's focus on listening to student voices helped me find courage to advocate, just as I did in the superintendent's student lunches. I hope every leader reading this book remembers that students can be partners in shaping what matters most.

Part 3
Refocus

In the ever-evolving landscape of educational leadership, the ability to pause, reflect, and recalibrate is critical. While relationships and results provide the foundation and structure for successful leadership, the act of reflection ensures sustainability and growth. Reflection allows leaders to step back from the noise of daily demands, examine their progress, and chart a course that aligns with their values and vision. This final section, Refocus, centers on the practices that enable leaders to pause, evaluate their priorities, and make intentional, informed decisions.

Refocus is not about slowing down; rather, it is about ensuring that every action has purpose, and every decision is grounded in clarity. The demands on educational leaders are immense—operational management, instructional leadership, staff development, stakeholder engagement, and more. These responsibilities require leaders to be constantly "on," navigating an environment that often prioritizes urgency over intentionality. Without deliberate time for reflection, leaders risk becoming trapped in cycles of reactivity, where the urgent consistently overshadows the important. By reclaiming time for what matters most, leaders can move beyond maintenance to transformation, focusing on long-term vision and meaningful progress.

Reflection is not an isolated act but an integral leadership skill. It is what allows leaders to connect their daily work to the larger mission of education. Through reflection, leaders can identify the barriers preventing progress, adjust strategies to meet evolving needs, and create systems that promote sustained success. It is in this intentional process that the seeds of innovation, growth, and resilience are sown.

This section explores the transformative power of reflection through three core themes: reclaiming time, leveraging technology, and fostering strategic thinking. Each chapter provides actionable insights into how leaders can redefine their time, optimize their tools, and align their priorities to lead with intentionality. These practices are not only about increasing efficiency but about finding clarity amid complexity. The stories and strategies shared here are not just theoretical—they are grounded in real-world experiences of balancing the competing demands of leadership while staying true to personal and professional values.

At the heart of refocus is the idea that leadership is not just about what you do, but about how and why you do it. Reflection allows leaders to align their actions with their core mission, ensuring that their efforts ripple outward to impact students, teachers, and the broader community. By carving out space to think deeply and act purposefully, leaders not only strengthen their own capacity but also create the conditions for others to thrive. This process builds a culture of intentionality across organizations, where everyone—from students to staff—feels empowered to contribute to shared goals.

Personal Reflection

In my own leadership journey, the practice of reflection has been transformative. Early in my career, I often found myself immersed in the day-to-day tasks of leadership, from managing operations to resolving immediate issues. While I was effective at keeping the ship afloat, I realized I was missing something essential: the opportunity to think strategically about the future. Over time, I began to prioritize moments of intentional reflection, carving out time to assess my priorities, consider long-term goals, and refocus my energy on what truly mattered. Whether it meant reclaiming time to be present with my family, leveraging tools like AI to streamline operations, or identifying the strategic moves that would create the greatest impact, these moments of reflection changed not just how I led but also the results I achieved.

One key lesson I've learned is that reflection is not a luxury—it is a necessity. It is the space where creativity flourishes, where leaders can reconnect with their purpose, and where solutions to complex problems emerge. Reflection allows leaders to step back, not as an escape from their work, but as a way to engage with it more fully. By creating intentional pauses in the relentless pace of leadership, we open ourselves to possibilities we might otherwise overlook.

Refocus is not about perfection; it's about progress. It is about embracing the idea that leadership is a dynamic process, requiring constant assessment, adjustment, and alignment. In a world that moves faster every day, the ability to pause and refocus is a superpower that enables leaders to create lasting, meaningful change. Leaders who prioritize reflection model this practice for others, creating a ripple effect that encourages intentionality throughout their organizations. Reflection is contagious—it inspires teams to pause, evaluate, and act with clarity and purpose.

For educational leaders, the ability to refocus also serves as a form of self-care. Leadership is demanding, often requiring significant mental and emotional energy. Without space for reflection, burnout becomes a real risk. Reflection offers leaders a chance to recharge, reconnect with their values, and approach their work with renewed energy. It's an investment not only in professional success but also in personal well-being.

As you journey through this section, you'll encounter strategies that highlight the power of reflection in reclaiming time, leveraging innovative tools, and fostering strategic thinking. The chapters will provide practical insights into how leaders can create space for intentionality and achieve greater impact in both their professional and personal lives. Through these practices, leaders can move beyond the immediate demands of their roles to focus on the transformative potential of their work.

As we transition into the final part of this book, remember that reflection is both a personal and professional act. It is the quiet yet powerful force that allows leaders to rise above the noise, connect with their mission, and guide their communities with clarity and strength. Reflection is the bridge between vision and action, enabling leaders to not only dream of what is possible but also make it a reality. May these reflections guide you as you continue to lead with intention, balance, and purpose, creating a ripple effect that extends far beyond your own work and touches the lives of those you serve.

14 The Leadership Time Dilemma

Time is the most valuable and finite resource in educational leadership, yet it's often mismanaged or consumed by urgent but low-impact tasks. The demands on school and district leaders are relentless: overseeing operations, managing crises, fostering relationships, advancing student achievement, responding to stakeholders, attending meetings, and navigating endless emails. These competing priorities often push leaders into a reactive cycle, leaving little room for strategic thinking, innovation, or personal well-being.

In education, time isn't just a resource—it's the foundation for achieving meaningful impact. Mismanaged time can derail even the best intentions, while well-managed time can drive transformational change. Understanding the leadership time dilemma requires examining how time gets consumed, its consequences, and how intentional time management can serve as a lever for educational excellence.

The Reality of Competing Demands

Educational leaders face a constant onslaught of demands. Consider a principal starting the school day with clear priorities but quickly being pulled into unexpected situations—a discipline issue in the cafeteria, a last-minute parent meeting, or an urgent facilities issue. Before long, the entire day has been consumed by immediate needs, leaving little progress on planned instructional goals or staff development.

Similarly, district superintendents are often expected to be "on call" for school boards, community groups, and administrative teams. One district leader shared, "I spend so much time responding to emails that I feel like I'm managing a customer service hotline rather than leading a district." These demands can leave little room for proactive work such as strategic planning, program development, or fostering community partnerships.

Leaders are also vulnerable to the "meeting trap." Hours are consumed by meetings—many of which lack clear outcomes or decision-making power. In some districts, leaders spend more than half of their week in meetings, often discussing the same issues repeatedly due to unclear action steps or accountability. One superintendent reflected that their district's progress stalled for months because they were "meeting about the same problems instead of solving them."

Example: Time Dilemma

My own experience as a first-year assistant principal in an urban high school mirrored these challenges. I quickly learned how stretched thin I was between student behavior incidents, overseeing duty spots, leading teacher PLCs, taking part in IEP meetings, creating a data room to track student achievement, completing classroom observations, and giving teachers feedback. For the first time ever, I felt I couldn't get everything done. I was spending too much time on so many different things that I wasn't doing anything well. I started to burn out.

Even experienced leaders aren't immune to this struggle. Whether in large urban districts or smaller rural settings, the pressure to balance competing demands can lead to prioritizing the urgent over the important. These cycles of reactivity perpetuate a culture of survival rather than progress.

The demands don't just stop with school administrators. At the district level, leaders often contend with issues ranging from facility repairs and vendor negotiations to managing public relations during community concerns. This multilayered responsibility highlights the challenge of triaging daily demands without losing sight of strategic objectives.

One often-overlooked issue is the cumulative effect of these demands on the mental health of educational leaders. Picture a typical Wednesday for a district principal: a facilities crisis at 7:00 a.m., a surprise staff absence at 8:00 a.m., an urgent parent meeting at 9:00 a.m., and a scheduled observation at 10:00 a.m.—all before lunchtime. By day's end, personal to-do lists remain untouched, fueling stress that compounds daily. The pressure to respond to crises, maintain visibility, and keep stakeholders satisfied leaves little room for leaders to decompress.

The result is often a cycle of reactivity, where leaders feel they are perpetually playing catch-up rather than proactively addressing systemic needs. Meetings get added to the calendar faster than they can be processed, emails pile up unanswered, and critical time for reflection and strategic planning evaporates under the weight of immediate demands. Beyond the professional toll, this constant strain seeps into personal life, leaving leaders mentally and emotionally exhausted, with little capacity to engage meaningfully with family, friends, or self-care.

This "day in the life" exemplifies why reclaiming time isn't just about better schedules or delegation—it's about protecting mental health and fostering sustainability. When leaders create space to step back and refocus, they regain the clarity and resilience needed to break free from the cycle of stress and reactivity. This intentional shift allows leaders to prioritize what truly matters, ensuring not only their well-being but also the effectiveness of their leadership.

The Cost of Mismanaged Time

The cost of mismanaged time is steep, impacting every level of the educational system. When leaders are overwhelmed with administrative tasks, student outcomes suffer as instructional leadership, one of the most critical roles of a school leader, is pushed aside. This often results in missed opportunities for coaching teachers, evaluating curriculum, and analyzing student data, which can ultimately lead to stagnant or declining academic performance.

Staff morale also declines when teachers feel unsupported due to leaders being inaccessible, overbooked, or disengaged from instructional priorities. A culture of constant crisis management can foster frustration and burnout among staff, who may begin to disengage when they see no consistent leadership presence or direction, ultimately affecting retention and adding further strain on leadership teams. Additionally, mismanaged time stifles innovation, forcing leaders into a survival-based model that prioritizes maintaining the status quo over adopting new programs, best practices, or creative solutions. This stagnation can widen the gap between innovative districts and those that merely maintain.

Burnout becomes inevitable for school leaders who lack effective time management, resulting in reduced effectiveness, strained relationships, and eventual turnover that disrupts school and district stability. Finally, missed opportunities for professional development, collaborative planning, and long-term improvement efforts limit the growth of both staff and students, preventing schools from reaching their full potential and stalling continuous improvement.

The Power of Well-Managed Time

In contrast, intentional time management empowers educational leaders to operate at their highest capacity. Consider a superintendent who blocks weekly "strategy sessions" to focus on long-term district goals or a principal who schedules "classroom walkthrough days" to observe instruction and provide actionable teacher feedback. These proactive practices build momentum for lasting improvements.

When I was an assistant principal experiencing burnout due to poor time management, I recognized the unsustainable pace I was maintaining. I began to delegate responsibilities where possible and implemented a better planning system that included time blocking. This shift allowed me to prioritize high-impact tasks while maintaining visibility and support for staff and students. It didn't eliminate the workload but enabled me to work more effectively and regain a sense of control over my time.

Leaders who manage their time well experience the following benefits:

Instructional Leadership Becomes Central

Time management allows leaders to prioritize classroom visits, curriculum planning, and teacher coaching. For example, a principal might designate mornings exclusively for classroom walkthroughs and coaching, while afternoons are reserved for operational tasks. By maintaining this balance, they can ensure a stronger focus on instruction. Teachers, in turn, feel supported, and students benefit from improved instructional quality.

A Culture of Support and Trust Develops

When leaders are visible and accessible, they foster trust among staff and students. A superintendent who carves out regular office hours to meet with teachers and staff demonstrates commitment to understanding their challenges and collaborating on solutions. This openness promotes a culture of mutual respect and shared accountability.

Strategic Goals Gain Traction

Protected time for planning allows leaders to set measurable goals and align resources accordingly. For instance, a district leader focused on literacy improvement might dedicate monthly time to analyze reading scores, meet with instructional coaches, and adjust strategies based on student performance. This consistency ensures progress toward long-term district objectives.

Innovative Programs Flourish

Innovation thrives when leaders have time to explore creative ideas and evaluate new initiatives. A principal might use dedicated brainstorming sessions with their leadership team to pilot programs like student mentoring or restorative practices. By intentionally allocating time for innovation, schools can implement transformative programs that benefit the entire community.

Leaders Reclaim Work-Life Balance

Intentional time management enables leaders to protect their personal time, reducing stress and preventing burnout. For example, a superintendent who prioritizes efficient meeting agendas and delegates tasks effectively can leave the office on time, setting a healthy work-life balance example for their staff. This balance not only improves their well-being but also models sustainable leadership practices for others.

Strategies for District Leaders

To address the leadership time dilemma, here are specific strategies for supporting students, teachers, and administrators. These strategies build on intentional time management practices to create a ripple effect across the entire school community.

For Students

- Maximize Learning Time: Limit disruptions to preserve instructional time. District leaders can establish policies that reduce unnecessary interruptions during class, such as consolidating announcements or improving scheduling for pull-out programs. Schools that prioritize uninterrupted blocks of learning often see improvements in student engagement and achievement.
- Equity-Focused Interventions: Leaders can identify at-risk students through data analysis and ensure resources are directed toward personalized supports. For instance, a district might allocate funds for after-school tutoring programs or hire intervention specialists to assist struggling students. These focused efforts can close achievement gaps and improve equity in learning opportunities.
- Student-Centered Scheduling: Schools can offer flexible schedules to meet diverse needs. For example, implementing study halls or independent learning periods can provide students with additional support for academic growth. Additionally, districts might explore hybrid or competency-based learning models that allow students to progress at their own pace, empowering them to take ownership of their education.

For Teachers

- Automate Administrative Tasks: Administrative burdens such as data entry, attendance tracking, or grading can be minimized through technology. Tools like grading software or AI-driven data analysis platforms reduce repetitive tasks, freeing teachers to focus on planning and instruction. Districts that invest in these tools not only save time for teachers but also improve accuracy and efficiency.
- Support Collaborative Planning: Leaders can prioritize time for teachers to collaborate on curriculum development and student data analysis. For example, scheduling weekly grade-level meetings or protected professional learning community (PLC) time helps teachers align their instruction with district priorities. This collaboration leads to more cohesive teaching strategies and improved student outcomes.

- Quick Decision-Making: Empower teachers to make decisions on non-critical issues without requiring multiple layers of approval. For instance, providing clear guidelines for classroom-level decisions—such as behavior management strategies—can reduce bottlenecks and improve teacher autonomy. Teachers who feel trusted are more likely to innovate and remain engaged in their work.

For Administrators

- Delegate Key Responsibilities: Leaders should empower assistant principals, department heads, or other administrators to manage specific portfolios. For example, a superintendent might delegate instructional leadership to a curriculum director while focusing on strategic planning and stakeholder relations. This division of responsibilities ensures that critical tasks are addressed without overloading one individual.
- Time-Saving Tech Tools: District leaders can implement scheduling software or communication platforms to streamline operations. For instance, using centralized platforms for staff communication, resource booking, or event scheduling eliminates redundancies and saves time across the district. AI-driven analytics tools can also assist administrators in identifying trends and making data-informed decisions quickly.
- Quarterly Leadership Reviews: Regularly scheduled leadership retreats or review sessions can help administrators assess progress on district goals and recalibrate as needed. These reviews provide dedicated time for reflection, ensuring alignment between daily operations and long-term objectives. For example, during these sessions, leaders can evaluate whether current initiatives are meeting-desired outcomes or require adjustments.

Educational leaders can't create more hours in the day, but they can reclaim their time by working smarter, not harder. By making intentional choices, setting clear priorities, and protecting time for what matters most, leaders can elevate their schools and districts from reactive management to proactive leadership that inspires staff, uplifts students, and drives lasting success. Time, when used wisely, becomes not just a tool, but a transformative force for educational progress.

15 Defining What Matters Most

In educational leadership, defining "what matters most" is both an art and a science. Leaders are pulled in countless directions by competing demands—student achievement, staff development, operational management, community relations, and policy mandates. Without a clear sense of priorities, leaders risk becoming reactive, addressing what feels urgent but not necessarily impactful. By defining core priorities, leaders can align efforts, resources, and energy toward meaningful, sustainable outcomes.

The Complexity of Defining Priorities

Educational leaders must navigate a web of complex and interconnected priorities. They balance day-to-day operations with long-term strategic planning, manage crises while fostering innovation, and support individual students while pursuing district-wide goals. The challenge lies in determining which tasks, initiatives, and responsibilities deserve the most attention.

A superintendent might face demands from school board members advocating for expanded programs, community groups seeking increased transparency, and teachers requesting more professional development. Similarly, a principal might be expected to raise test scores, enhance school culture, and manage a dwindling budget—all simultaneously. Leaders can easily become consumed by trying to do everything at once, often at the expense of doing what truly matters well.

Defining priorities can feel overwhelming, especially in high-stakes environments where decisions impact students, staff, and the broader community. For instance, balancing immediate operational concerns—like filling staff vacancies or managing building repairs—with strategic goals, such as improving equity in advanced coursework, often leaves leaders feeling pulled in conflicting directions. This tension underscores the importance of clear decision-making frameworks.

The Danger of Undefined Priorities

The danger of undefined priorities in educational leadership can lead to significant challenges that impact the entire organization. Without a clear sense of purpose, leaders often pursue too many initiatives simultaneously, resulting in fragmented focus. This dilution of effort prevents any single initiative from gaining enough momentum to succeed, leading to "initiative fatigue" that frustrates both leaders and their teams.

Additionally, the absence of clear priorities contributes to decision fatigue, as leaders constantly switch between unrelated tasks, eroding mental energy and lowering productivity. Over time, this cycle increases stress and leads to burnout, limiting a leader's capacity to inspire and support their teams. Ineffective resource allocation is another consequence, with limited time, funding, and staff capacity often spread too thin, undermining the success of critical programs.

Finally, when leaders frequently change direction or pursue conflicting goals, trust and credibility with stakeholders erode, causing staff and community members to become disengaged and making it harder to gain support for future initiatives. These challenges underscore the importance of defining and communicating clear priorities to ensure alignment across all levels of the organization.

What Matters Most: A Framework for Prioritization

Defining "what matters most" in educational leadership involves a thoughtful and reflective process rooted in three essential questions. The first question asks what is most aligned with the mission and vision of the school or district. While many educational institutions have mission statements, their true power lies in how leaders use them as guideposts for decision-making. Initiatives should directly support the mission. For instance, if a district's mission emphasizes equity and student achievement, efforts to address opportunity gaps or provide differentiated instruction should take priority over less mission-critical projects.

Another key consideration is determining what will have the greatest impact on students. Student outcomes must always be at the heart of decision-making, with leaders prioritizing programs that have a proven track record of improving student learning. This could include literacy interventions, access to advanced coursework, or social-emotional supports that foster well-rounded development.

Sustainability is crucial for long-term success. Leaders must evaluate whether initiatives can be maintained with available resources and staffing. Programs reliant on temporary grants or unsustainable workloads should be reconsidered or restructured to ensure they can be supported over time. These guiding questions provide educational leaders with a clear decision-making framework, ensuring that resources and efforts are consistently focused on initiatives that truly matter.

Case Study: A Superintendent's Decision-Making Framework

A superintendent in a mid-sized district found themselves at a crossroads, navigating a complex web of stakeholder demands that included the school board's push for expanding STEM programs, community members' passionate advocacy for enhanced arts education, and parents' growing concerns over school safety. Recognizing that pursuing all three initiatives simultaneously would stretch the district's resources too thin, the superintendent embarked on a thoughtful, deliberate process to establish a clear decision-making framework that would guide the district's next steps.

Central to this framework was a commitment to aligning any new initiatives with the district's mission: preparing students for college and career readiness. While all three areas were important, the superintendent reflected deeply on which initiatives would most directly support this mission. STEM education, with its growing importance in the modern workforce, and school safety, as a fundamental prerequisite for effective learning, stood out as the strongest fits. This alignment ensured that the district's core purpose remained at the forefront of every decision.

In addition to alignment, the superintendent prioritized evidence of impact. They examined data from neighboring districts that had successfully expanded their STEM offerings, noting a significant increase in post-secondary enrollment rates among students. This data provided compelling evidence that investing in STEM could have lasting benefits for students, giving them the skills and opportunities needed to succeed beyond high school. The superintendent also considered the voices of parents who, while supportive of academic enrichment, were increasingly vocal about the need for safer school environments. Research underscored that students learn best when they feel safe, further reinforcing the importance of addressing school safety as a priority.

Sustainability was the final, critical criterion. The superintendent understood that even the most promising initiatives would falter without long-term financial support. After careful exploration of funding options, they secured grant funding specifically for school safety upgrades. This financial backing ensured that enhancing safety measures would not divert resources from other essential programs, creating a balanced, sustainable path forward.

By taking the time to define priorities clearly and transparently, the superintendent not only gained the approval of the school board but also earned the trust and support of the broader community. This thoughtful approach resulted in significant, measurable improvements in student outcomes within two years, illustrating the power of strategic, mission-driven decision-making in educational leadership.

Personal Example

In my school district, we faced a challenge with undefined student outcome goals. Without a clear framework, decisions often reflected individual priorities rather than the district's mission. Recognizing the need for clarity, my board and I embarked on a process to define specific, measurable student outcome goals.

This collaborative effort included engaging stakeholders to identify what mattered most for our students' success. Once these goals were established, we aligned our resources and efforts accordingly. Today, when financial decisions arise, we weigh them against these outcome goals: Do they align with what we've identified as critical for student success?

This process not only clarified my focus as a superintendent but also brought consistency to decision-making. Whether it's a request from another administrator, a board member, or a community stakeholder, I have a clear lens through which to evaluate priorities, ensuring alignment with our shared vision.

Additionally, having clearly defined student outcome goals approved by the board provides a stabilizing force for the district in times of leadership transition. Whether board members or superintendents change, these goals serve as a consistent framework for decision-making and strategic planning. They create a shared understanding of what the district is striving to achieve, reducing the risk of sudden shifts in priorities and ensuring that student success remains at the forefront. This continuity is critical for maintaining momentum and trust within the community, even as leadership evolves.

The Role of Communication in Defining Priorities

Once priorities are established, leaders must communicate them clearly and consistently. Staff, families, and community stakeholders need to understand why specific goals matter most and how their efforts contribute to achieving them. Transparency builds trust and fosters shared accountability.

Effective communication also involves creating feedback loops where stakeholders can share their perspectives. This ensures that priorities remain relevant and adaptable to changing circumstances. For example, a district may initially focus on literacy initiatives but later expand to include mental health supports based on community feedback.

Defining "what matters most" isn't a one-time exercise; it's a continuous process requiring reflection, assessment, and recalibration. When leaders anchor their decisions in mission-driven priorities, they create clarity, focus, and momentum. With a shared understanding of what truly matters, school communities can work together with purpose and resolve, achieving outcomes that transform lives.

Strategies for District Leaders

To help educational leaders define and pursue what matters most, consider these strategies aligned with students, teachers, and administrators. Expanded details illustrate how these strategies can be applied effectively.

For Students

- Student-Centered Initiatives: Programs like mentoring, career readiness, and enrichment activities are critical to enhancing student experiences and outcomes. For example, implementing a peer mentoring program can help younger students build confidence and adjust to new environments, while older students develop leadership skills. Districts can also partner with local businesses to create internships that expose students to real-world applications of their learning.
- Equity-Focused Policies: Decisions must address opportunity gaps and provide equitable access to resources. For instance, districts can adopt policies ensuring that all students have access to advanced coursework, technology, and extracurricular activities, regardless of socioeconomic status. This might involve providing laptops for students who lack devices at home or subsidizing fees for participation in sports or arts programs.
- Wellness Supports: Allocating time and funding for mental health services is a core priority for student well-being. Districts might hire additional school counselors, establish partnerships with local mental health organizations, or create dedicated wellness centers on campus. These efforts can help reduce barriers to learning by addressing issues like anxiety, trauma, or bullying that may otherwise go unaddressed.

For Teachers

- Clear Instructional Priorities: Aligning curriculum, assessment, and professional development with district-wide goals helps teachers stay focused and effective. For example, if a district prioritizes literacy, leaders can provide ongoing training in evidence-based reading strategies and ensure that classroom resources are aligned with this focus.

- Collaborative Planning Time: Carving out protected time for teachers to work together fosters collaboration and consistency. Structured professional learning communities (PLCs) can be used to analyze student data, share best practices, and plan interdisciplinary lessons. Districts might also consider scheduling common planning periods for grade-level or subject-area teams to ensure that collaboration becomes a routine part of the workweek.
- Reduced Administrative Burden: Streamlining tasks like attendance reporting or grade submission frees teachers to focus on instruction. For example, using a centralized online platform for routine administrative tasks can significantly reduce the time teachers spend on paperwork. Additionally, simplifying district reporting requirements can alleviate stress and allow teachers to dedicate more time to their students.

For Administrators

- Goal-Setting Frameworks: Strategic planning tools help administrators establish clear, measurable goals aligned with district priorities. For example, a principal might use a dashboard to track progress on school improvement goals, such as increasing student attendance or improving test scores. By regularly reviewing this data with their leadership team, they can make timely adjustments to ensure progress.
- Data-Driven Decision-Making: Administrators can leverage technology to analyze trends and make informed decisions. For instance, using analytics tools to monitor attendance, behavior incidents, and academic performance enables leaders to identify patterns and address issues proactively. These insights ensure that interventions are targeted and impactful.
- Accountability Systems: Transparent systems for tracking and reporting progress help administrators maintain focus and ensure alignment with district goals. For example, a superintendent might hold quarterly progress reviews with principals, during which they discuss milestones, challenges, and next steps. These meetings create a shared sense of accountability and encourage collaboration across schools.

Defining "what matters most" in educational leadership requires a deliberate focus on aligning efforts with a school or district's core mission, ensuring that decisions prioritize student success, and maintaining sustainability for long-term impact. Without clear priorities, leaders risk spreading resources too thin and losing sight of what truly drives progress. Establishing a framework for prioritization—considering mission alignment, impact on students, and feasibility—helps leaders make informed choices and navigate competing demands effectively. Communication plays a crucial role in reinforcing priorities, building stakeholder trust, and fostering shared accountability. When leaders clearly define and communicate what matters most, they create a culture of focus, intentionality, and continuous improvement, ensuring that their schools and districts remain resilient and responsive to the evolving needs of students and the broader educational community.

16 Delegation and Empowerment

Delegation is one of the most vital skills for effective leadership, yet it is often one of the most difficult to master. Many educational leaders enter the field as high achievers, accustomed to solving problems themselves and taking pride in their ability to get things done. However, as the scope of responsibilities grows—from managing classrooms to leading schools and districts—leaders quickly discover that trying to do everything themselves is not only unsustainable but also counterproductive. True leadership lies in empowering others to take ownership and lead in their respective roles.

Delegation isn't just about getting tasks off a leader's plate; it's about building capacity within the organization. When leaders effectively delegate, they create a culture of trust, shared accountability, and collective growth. This chapter explores the challenges, benefits, and strategies of delegation in educational leadership.

The Misconceptions About Delegation

Many leaders view delegation as giving up control or admitting weakness, leading to micromanagement or an overburdened leader who struggles to prioritize high-impact tasks. One common barrier to effective delegation is perfectionism—the belief that "no one else can do it as well as I can." This mindset often stems from a fear of mistakes or a desire to maintain high standards. While these intentions are understandable, they can create a bottleneck in decision-making and limit the growth of team members. For instance, a principal who insists on reviewing every school newsletter themselves may prevent staff from developing their skills while also wasting valuable time that could be better spent on strategic leadership tasks.

Another barrier is a lack of trust, where leaders fear that others won't follow through or meet expectations. Trust is essential for effective delegation, but leaders who struggle with trust often hover over delegated tasks or take them back at the first sign of trouble. This approach not only undermines staff morale but also creates a cycle where employees feel disempowered and disengaged. A district leader who refuses to delegate curriculum planning to an instructional coach, for example, may miss out on innovative ideas and valuable insights from those closer to the instructional process.

Short-term thinking is also a significant challenge. Many leaders assume that it's faster to do something themselves rather than invest time in training someone else. While initial training may take time, the long-term benefits of delegation far outweigh the short-term inconvenience. Teaching a secretary to manage scheduling software, for instance, might require an upfront investment of time, but it ultimately saves hours and increases efficiency in the long run.

By addressing these misconceptions, leaders can break free from habits that hinder their effectiveness and foster a culture of trust and empowerment within their organizations. Delegation is not about relinquishing control but about building capacity, developing talent, and ensuring that leadership efforts are focused where they matter most.

The Benefits of Delegation

Delegation, when done effectively, has far-reaching benefits for leaders, staff, and the entire organization. Each of the following benefits illustrates how delegation transforms both individuals and the organization.

Increased Leadership Focus

Delegation allows leaders to focus on high-level responsibilities such as strategic planning, instructional leadership, and community engagement. For example, a superintendent who delegates daily operational tasks to their cabinet can dedicate time to meeting with legislators about education policy or attending to long-term district initiatives. This focus ensures that leaders can address systemic issues rather than getting bogged down by day-to-day details.

Capacity Building

By delegating tasks, leaders empower staff to develop new skills, take on leadership roles, and grow professionally. A principal who assigns teachers to lead professional learning communities not only reduces their own workload but also provides those teachers with opportunities to enhance their facilitation and leadership skills. Over time, this builds a pipeline of future leaders within the organization.

Improved Decision-Making

When responsibilities are shared, decision-making becomes more collaborative and informed, drawing on the diverse expertise of the team. For instance, delegating the responsibility of analyzing student performance data to a team of teachers and instructional coaches can result in more nuanced and actionable strategies to improve learning outcomes. This collective approach ensures that decisions are grounded in varied perspectives and expertise.

Better Work-Life Balance

Leaders who delegate effectively are less likely to experience burnout, enabling them to maintain energy and clarity. A district leader who trusts their team to manage day-to-day operations can confidently leave work at a reasonable hour, knowing that their school or district is in capable hands. This balance not only improves the leader's well-being but also sets a positive example for staff and students.

Personal Example: Learning to Let Go

Early in my career as an assistant principal, I believed that doing everything myself was the key to being an effective leader. I thought my capability to handle multiple tasks demonstrated competence and reliability. Whether it was managing student discipline, organizing events, or creating data reports, I was determined to take it all on.

As I moved into roles as a principal and eventually as a superintendent, I quickly realized that this approach was unsustainable. Not only was I overextending myself, but I was also missing opportunities to develop the leadership capacity of those around me. Delegation became a necessity.

Now, I consistently use delegation as a tool to empower my team. For example, I assign teachers to lead professional learning communities, empower principals to oversee specific initiatives, and collaborate with board members to tackle district-wide projects. Delegation allows me to focus on strategic leadership while fostering a culture where everyone takes ownership of their work. It's not about giving up control—it's about sharing responsibility and growing together as a team.

The Principles of Effective Delegation

Effective delegation is a deliberate process that involves more than simply assigning tasks; it requires clear communication, trust, and ongoing support. Defining roles and expectations is essential to successful delegation. Leaders must clearly articulate what needs to be done, who is responsible, and what the desired outcomes are. Written guidelines or checklists can help clarify expectations and ensure accountability. For example, when delegating the organization of a school event, a principal might outline specific deliverables, deadlines, and decision-making authority, leaving little room for confusion or misinterpretation.

Matching tasks to strengths is another critical principle. Assigning tasks based on individuals' skills, interests, and potential for growth increases the likelihood of success and engagement. A superintendent might delegate a financial analysis task to a business manager with expertise in budgeting, while assigning the development of a new teacher mentoring program to an instructional coach who is passionate about professional development. This thoughtful alignment ensures that tasks are completed efficiently and with enthusiasm.

Providing support and resources is equally important. Leaders must ensure that those taking on delegated tasks have the tools, training, and guidance they need to succeed. For instance, when assigning a teacher to lead a Professional Learning Community (PLC), a school leader might provide professional development in facilitation skills and access to relevant data or instructional materials. This support not only builds confidence but also fosters trust between leaders and their teams.

Effective delegation requires regular follow-up and feedback. Checking in periodically offers an opportunity to provide support, recognize accomplishments, and ensure accountability without micromanaging. For example, a district leader who delegates the development of a new literacy initiative might schedule biweekly progress meetings to offer guidance, celebrate milestones, and collaboratively address challenges. These principles, when practiced consistently, create a culture where delegation is seen as an opportunity for growth and shared leadership.

Delegation and empowerment are not about leaders doing less but about enabling others to do more. By sharing responsibility and fostering a culture of trust, leaders can elevate their teams, focus on their core priorities, and create a thriving school or district environment. True leadership is not measured by how much one can accomplish alone but by the collective success of the team. When leaders delegate effectively, they unlock the full potential of their organization and create lasting impact.

Strategies for District Leaders

To foster a culture of delegation and empowerment, consider these strategies aligned with students, teachers, and administrators:

For Students

- Student Leadership Opportunities: Create roles for students to take ownership of school culture, such as leading clubs, organizing events, or serving on advisory councils. For example, students serving on a district's equity council can provide valuable insights into improving inclusivity while developing their own leadership skills.
- Peer Tutoring Programs: Empower students to support each other academically, fostering a collaborative learning environment. A structured peer tutoring program can boost confidence for both tutors and tutees, leading to improved academic performance and stronger school community bonds.
- Student-Led Conferences: Allow students to take the lead in presenting their academic progress to parents and teachers. This practice encourages self-reflection and accountability while helping students develop communication and presentation skills.

Districts that adopt this strategy often report increased student engagement and parent involvement.

For Teachers

- Shared Leadership Models: Assign teachers to lead professional learning communities, curriculum teams, or special projects. For example, giving a group of teachers the responsibility to design a district-wide STEM curriculum ensures that those closest to the classroom have a voice in decision-making, resulting in more relevant and practical outcomes.
- Mentorship Opportunities: Pair veteran teachers with newer staff to build relationships and share expertise. This approach not only supports novice teachers but also provides experienced educators with leadership opportunities. Districts with formal mentorship programs often see higher retention rates among new hires.
- Classroom Autonomy: Empower teachers to design and implement innovative instructional strategies that align with district goals. For instance, a district might encourage teachers to pilot project-based learning approaches, allowing them to tailor instruction to their students' unique needs and interests while aligning with broader curricular objectives.

For Administrators

- Distributed Leadership: Delegate key responsibilities, such as overseeing programs or managing specific initiatives, to assistant principals or directors. For example, an assistant principal might take ownership of student discipline policies, freeing the principal to focus on instructional leadership.
- Capacity-Building Initiatives: Provide training and opportunities for administrators to take on higher-level responsibilities. For instance, a superintendent might organize a leadership academy for aspiring principals, equipping them with the skills needed to take on greater challenges within the district.
- Collaborative Decision-Making: Involve administrators in strategic planning processes to ensure shared ownership of district goals.

For example, inviting building principals to co-create the district's strategic plan fosters a sense of investment and ensures that goals are grounded in the realities of individual schools.

Effective delegation and empowerment are foundational to sustainable leadership, allowing educational leaders to build capacity within their organizations while focusing on high-impact priorities. Delegation is not about relinquishing control but about developing others, fostering shared ownership, and ensuring that leadership responsibilities are distributed effectively. When leaders clearly define expectations, match tasks to strengths, provide necessary support, and maintain open communication, they create an environment where staff and students feel trusted, valued, and capable of contributing meaningfully. Empowering others strengthens decision-making, enhances innovation, and fosters a culture of collaboration. Ultimately, leaders who delegate effectively not only improve efficiency and engagement but also cultivate the next generation of leaders, ensuring long-term success for their schools and districts.

17 Leveraging Technology and AI

Technology and AI have rapidly evolved, offering school leaders tools to streamline operations and personalize learning experiences. From automating attendance to analyzing data for equity gaps, these solutions free us to focus on relationships and results. However, many leaders struggle to identify the most effective ways to leverage these tools amid the ever-expanding array of options. By thoughtfully integrating technology and AI into daily practices, district leaders can free up time for strategic initiatives while improving outcomes for students, teachers, and administrators. This chapter explores the transformative potential of AI and technology in education, highlighting specific strategies for using these tools to maximize efficiency and impact.

The Role of Technology and AI in Education

AI and technology provide solutions to many of the challenges educational leaders face. From automating administrative tasks to personalizing student learning experiences, these tools can revolutionize how schools and districts operate. Yet, their implementation must be intentional, with a focus on aligning technological capabilities with the district's mission and goals.

Technology in education has evolved significantly, from basic attendance tracking systems to sophisticated platforms that analyze data in real time. AI, as the next frontier, has the potential to transform decision-making by providing leaders with actionable insights at unprecedented speeds. For example, tools powered by AI can identify trends in attendance or achievement gaps, allowing leaders to intervene before problems escalate. This level of precision can help align resources with district priorities, ensuring that every decision supports the mission of improving student outcomes.

When implemented thoughtfully, AI enhances—not replaces—human judgment. It provides leaders with the tools to work smarter and focus on what matters most: fostering relationships, driving results, and creating equitable opportunities for all students.

Benefits of Leveraging Technology and AI

Leveraging technology and AI offers numerous benefits that can transform educational leadership and operations. One of the most significant advantages is time savings. Automation reduces the burden of repetitive tasks, allowing leaders to focus on high-priority initiatives. Tools like email filters and automated scheduling systems free up hours previously spent on administrative work. For example, a district leader who automates meeting invitations, follow-ups, and agenda distributions can redirect that time toward strategic efforts such as curriculum planning or engaging with stakeholders.

Another critical benefit is the ability to make data-driven decisions. AI-powered analytics provide valuable insights into student performance, resource allocation, and operational efficiency. Predictive analytics tools, for instance, can forecast enrollment changes, helping districts prepare for shifts in staffing or classroom needs. Similarly, AI tools can analyze standardized test scores to identify areas where students are struggling, enabling targeted interventions that improve outcomes.

Personalized learning is also enhanced through adaptive technologies that tailor instruction to meet individual student needs. Programs like Lexia or DreamBox adjust in real time based on student responses, creating personalized learning pathways that keep students engaged and on track. These tools allow districts to support diverse learners, from those needing remediation to advanced students seeking enrichment.

Improved communication is another benefit of leveraging technology and AI. Automated messaging systems and chatbots streamline communication with families and staff. For instance, a chatbot can provide instant answers to common parent questions about bus schedules, meal plans, or school policies, reducing the workload on administrative staff. Additionally, automated messaging platforms enable leaders to send consistent and timely updates, fostering transparency and trust within the school community.

Finally, technology promotes equity and access by bridging gaps for underserved students and schools. Districts that distribute internet hotspots or loaner devices ensure that all students, regardless of socioeconomic status, have access to online learning. AI tools can also help identify resource disparities, allowing leaders to allocate funds where they are needed most, ensuring every student has the opportunity to succeed.

Personal Example: Streamlining Communications with AI

As a superintendent, I've found that integrating AI into my own workflows has been a game-changer, helping me manage the diverse and demanding responsibilities of district leadership. While these tools haven't yet been widely adopted across my district, they have significantly improved my personal efficiency in key areas.

For example, AI-powered tools have streamlined communication tasks. Whether it's drafting district-level social media updates or creating comprehensive documents like employee handbooks, I've saved hours of time that would otherwise be spent formatting, organizing, and editing. These tools allow me to communicate effectively and professionally while focusing on higher-priority tasks.

AI has also been invaluable in supporting curriculum planning. By using these tools to align curriculum resources with state standards, I've been able to assist instructional leaders in organizing unit plans more efficiently. While this doesn't replace the essential work teachers do, it lightens their load and ensures alignment with key instructional goals.

Additionally, AI has enhanced how I approach data analysis. From tracking trends in attendance to identifying areas for improvement, these tools help me process and interpret large amounts of data quickly. This saves time and allows me to make informed decisions more effectively. While these advancements reflect my personal use of AI rather than district-wide implementation, they demonstrate the potential for these tools to save time and enhance focus, enabling leaders like me to prioritize what matters most.

Overcoming Barriers to Adoption

While the potential of AI in education is immense, its integration is not without challenges. One significant barrier is resistance to change. Staff may feel intimidated by new tools or fear that AI could threaten their job security. Overcoming this resistance requires clear communication about the purpose of AI tools: to enhance and support educators' work, not replace it. Implementing pilot programs can help ease these fears by allowing staff to experiment with and understand the tools before full-scale implementation, fostering a sense of involvement and ownership in the process.

Cost constraints also present a challenge, as many AI solutions require significant upfront investment. However, districts can mitigate these costs by pursuing grants or forming partnerships with technology companies. Many companies offer discounted rates or funding opportunities for educational institutions willing to participate in pilot programs or research initiatives, making AI integration more financially feasible.

A lack of training is another common obstacle. Without adequate professional development, staff may struggle to use AI tools effectively. Districts can address this by offering hands-on workshops, establishing peer coaching programs, and providing continuous support as staff integrate AI into their workflows. Ensuring that educators feel competent and confident in using these tools is essential for successful adoption.

Equity concerns must also be prioritized during AI integration. Ensuring all students and staff have access to technology and resources is critical to avoid exacerbating existing disparities. Districts should focus on equitable distribution of devices, internet access, and training. For example, one rural district successfully partnered with a local telecom provider to expand broadband access to underserved areas, ensuring all students could benefit from online learning opportunities.

Overcoming these barriers requires intentional planning, stakeholder buy-in, and a steadfast commitment to equity. By addressing these challenges thoughtfully, districts can unlock the full potential of AI to enhance learning and improve operational efficiency.

Strategies for District Leaders

To harness the power of AI and technology, district leaders can implement strategies tailored to students, teachers, and administrators:

For Students

- Personalized Learning Platforms: Tools like Naviance or adaptive assessment programs meet students where they are and guide them toward their goals. These platforms can identify gaps in understanding and provide targeted resources, ensuring every student progresses at their own pace.
- Equity through Technology: Providing devices, internet access, and digital tools ensures all students can benefit from technological advancements. For example, a district that equips every student with a Chromebook levels the playing field for students in low-income communities.
- Digital Citizenship Programs: Teaching students how to use technology responsibly prepares them for success in an increasingly digital world. Topics like online safety, privacy, and ethical use of AI tools ensure students can navigate the complexities of the digital age.

For Teachers

- Automating Administrative Tasks: Automated grading systems like Gradescope or lesson plan generators reduce teachers' workloads. These tools allow teachers to focus more on instruction and less on repetitive tasks, improving both efficiency and morale.
- Data Insights for Instruction: AI tools can analyze student performance data, helping teachers identify trends and tailor their approaches. For example, dashboards that highlight struggling students enable teachers to provide timely interventions.
- Professional Development: Training on emerging technologies equips teachers to integrate AI effectively into their classrooms. Workshops on AI-powered tools like ChatGPT for lesson planning or Canva for creating visual aids inspire teachers to innovate and enhance engagement.

For Administrators

- Operational Efficiencies: AI-driven systems for scheduling, budgeting, and resource management streamline daily operations. For example, scheduling software that optimizes bus routes can save districts both time and money.
- Data Dashboards: Aggregating and visualizing district-wide data supports informed decision-making. Dashboards can display real-time attendance rates, test scores, or funding allocations, enabling leaders to act proactively.
- Enhanced Communication Tools: AI-powered platforms enable timely and effective communication with families, staff, and community stakeholders. Tools that automatically translate messages into multiple languages improve inclusivity and ensure all stakeholders stay informed.

AI and technology are not merely tools for efficiency—they are catalysts for innovation and equity. Emerging trends like predictive analytics for enrollment planning and virtual reality for immersive learning experiences demonstrate the transformative potential of these tools. Educational leaders must adopt a mindset of continual reflection, ensuring that technology aligns with their mission and addresses community needs. When used thoughtfully, AI enables leaders to refocus on their most important work: fostering relationships, driving results, and creating opportunities for every student to thrive.

18 Creating Space for Reflection and Strategic Thinking

In the fast-paced world of educational leadership, it can be tempting to focus solely on immediate tasks and crises. However, one of the most critical aspects of effective leadership is creating space for reflection and strategic thinking. Without time to evaluate progress, consider long-term goals, and make intentional plans, leaders risk merely keeping things afloat rather than driving meaningful change.

Reflection is not a luxury—it's a necessity. It allows leaders to recalibrate, refocus, and innovate. This chapter explores how carving out time for reflection and strategic thinking can elevate leadership effectiveness and ultimately transform schools and districts.

The Leadership Challenge: Balancing Urgency and Intentionality

Educational leaders often juggle an overwhelming array of responsibilities, from managing daily operations to addressing staff and community concerns. These immediate demands can leave little room for the deeper work of planning and innovation. Leaders may find themselves caught in a cycle of reactive decision-making, where long-term visioning takes a back seat to short-term survival.

This challenge is further compounded by the constant influx of unexpected issues—student discipline concerns, staffing shortages, or emergency facility repairs—that require immediate attention. In such environments, even well-intentioned leaders can find their days consumed by crises, leaving little time to step back and consider broader priorities. When our district leadership team meets biweekly, we always start our meeting with a reflection time. Each principal shares a success and a challenge. While brief, this reflection time anchors us in continuous improvement and keep us connected amidst the chaos. Without dedicated time for reflection, leaders risk operating in maintenance mode, where the focus is on keeping systems running rather than driving meaningful progress.

Research on time management in leadership emphasizes the "tyranny of the urgent," where pressing but less impactful tasks overshadow strategic initiatives. This imbalance is particularly pronounced in education, where the stakes are high, and the pace is unrelenting. However, creating space for intentional reflection is not about ignoring urgent needs but about ensuring that daily actions align with a broader vision. This balance is what enables leaders to transform reactive moments into proactive opportunities.

Personal Example: Moving Beyond Survival Mode

As the superintendent of a small, rural district, I've faced my share of challenges in balancing daily responsibilities with long-term planning. For several years, I held the dual role of superintendent and high school principal. While I managed both roles effectively for a time, I eventually realized a critical truth: although I was keeping the district running, that was all I was doing.

I didn't have the bandwidth to reflect on where we were as a district, let alone think intentionally about where we needed to go. My focus was entirely on operational tasks, from addressing immediate student needs to managing staff schedules. Reflection and purposeful planning—the key components of moving our district forward—were absent.

Recognizing this gap, I made the case to my school board to split the positions, allowing me to focus solely on the role of superintendent. Once my role was split, I could focus on the big goals our district had set and keeping our team aligned and on track with those goals. This shift allowed me to implement goal tracking systems, align resources more effectively, and make necessary course adjustments when needed.

One of the most significant outcomes of this transition was helping our board adopt student outcome goals. Each month, I now guide the board in tracking progress toward these goals, ensuring that we stay focused on what matters most: our students. This structured approach to monitoring and alignment has not only improved our decision-making but also strengthened the board's commitment to long-term success.

This shift from survival mode to strategic leadership marked a turning point for our district. It allowed us to move beyond maintaining the status quo and instead focus on creating a better future, one rooted in intentionality, reflection, and shared accountability.

The Benefits of Reflection and Strategic Thinking

Making time for reflection and strategic thinking offers far-reaching benefits for leaders and their organizations. One of the most significant advantages is gaining clarity on priorities. Reflection allows leaders to identify what matters most and ensures that daily efforts align with long-term objectives. For instance, a district leader might use reflective time to reassess how resources are allocated, ensuring that every decision supports the district's mission. This clarity helps leaders focus their energy on initiatives that have the greatest impact, fostering a more purpose-driven approach to leadership.

Strategic thinking also enhances decision-making by providing leaders with the time to evaluate options thoroughly, anticipate challenges, and make well-informed choices. A superintendent planning a major facilities upgrade, for example, might use reflective time to gather input from stakeholders, analyze financial data, and consider long-term implications. This thoughtful approach leads to decisions that are both innovative and fiscally responsible, balancing immediate needs with future goals.

Another key benefit is fostering innovation. Stepping back from the day-to-day demands of leadership allows leaders to explore creative solutions and implement forward-thinking initiatives. For instance, reflecting on teacher feedback could inspire the development of a professional development program tailored to specific needs, ultimately improving both staff morale and instructional quality. Innovation thrives when leaders have the mental space to think beyond routine operations.

Finally, reflection strengthens resilience by providing leaders with opportunities to recharge and refocus. Taking time for self-reflection helps prevent burnout and ensures that leaders maintain the energy needed to navigate the complexities of their roles. Leaders who prioritize reflective practices often report feeling more grounded, balanced, and prepared to face challenges with confidence and clarity.

The Habits of Reflective Leaders

Building time for reflection and strategic thinking into a leadership routine requires intentional effort. One effective practice is scheduling dedicated "thinking time." Blocking out regular, uninterrupted periods for reflection and planning ensures that strategic thinking remains a priority. Treating this time as non-negotiable—much like a critical meeting—allows leaders to review district goals, analyze progress, and brainstorm solutions to challenges without the distractions of daily operational demands.

Conducting leadership retrospectives is another valuable habit. After major events or decisions, taking the time to evaluate what worked, what didn't, and what could be improved provides an opportunity for continuous learning. For example, after implementing a new district initiative, a retrospective might reveal key adjustments needed for greater success in the future. This practice encourages leaders to refine their approach and build on previous experiences.

Seeking outside perspectives can also enhance reflective leadership. Engaging in executive coaching, peer networks, or professional learning communities provides new insights and ideas. Collaboration with other leaders fosters creative problem-solving and offers valuable feedback on strategic plans. Discussing challenges with peers who have faced similar situations can lead to innovative solutions and a broader understanding of complex issues.

Finally, practicing mindfulness can support clarity and focus. Incorporating mindfulness techniques such as meditation, journaling, or deep breathing exercises can help leaders manage stress and enhance their ability to think critically. Even brief mindfulness practices allow leaders to step back from the constant demands of their roles and approach challenges with a refreshed perspective. By integrating these habits, reflective leaders can cultivate greater strategic awareness, improve decision-making, and create a more thoughtful approach to leadership.

Strategies for District Leaders

To create space for reflection and strategic thinking, district leaders can implement strategies tailored to students, teachers, and administrators:

For Students

- Model Reflective Practices: Introduce district-wide "pause" days where students engage in self-assessment and goal-setting activities. This practice encourages students to reflect on their progress and set meaningful goals for improvement.
- Encourage Ownership of Learning: Provide students with tools like digital portfolios to track their work over time, fostering accountability and self-directed growth.
- Student-Led Projects: Empower students to take on leadership roles in projects, allowing them to reflect on their contributions and learning outcomes. For instance, a student-led community service project can highlight the importance of planning, collaboration, and reflection.

For Teachers

- Collaborative Reflection Time: Build teacher-led professional learning communities (PLCs) that focus on reflective teaching and shared problem-solving. Structured discussions can lead to actionable changes in instructional practices.
- Structured Planning Days: Allocate time for teachers to step back from daily instruction and focus on long-term planning. These days can be used to align lesson plans with district goals or to develop new instructional strategies.
- Supportive Feedback Loops: Encourage teachers to analyze classroom data and use insights to adjust their instructional practices. This reflective process ensures that teaching strategies remain effective and responsive.

For Administrators

- Leadership Retreats: Organize regular retreats where administrators can reflect on district progress, share insights, and collaboratively set future priorities. These retreats foster a culture of alignment and shared accountability.
- Strategic Planning Tools: Provide administrators with frameworks like SWOT analysis or goal-setting templates to help map out initiatives and align them with district objectives.
- Regular Progress Reviews: Establish routines for administrators to assess their work, celebrate successes, and recalibrate where necessary. These reviews ensure that the district remains on track toward its long-term goals.

The Impact of Intentional Leadership

Creating space for reflection and strategic thinking is about more than personal growth—it's about empowering your organization to reach its full potential. A leader can only drive meaningful change when he or she takes the time to step back, evaluate, and plan with purpose. For me, the decision to step away from dual roles and focus solely on being a superintendent transformed how I approached leadership. It allowed me to move beyond survival mode and focus on building a better future for our district. The same is possible for any leader who prioritizes reflection and strategic thinking, unlocking the potential for innovation, alignment, and growth.

19 The Ripple Effect of Reclaimed Time

Reclaiming time as a leader is not just about improving operational efficiency or achieving professional goals—it's about creating space for what matters most in life. For many educational leaders, the ripple effects of better time management extend beyond the workplace, influencing relationships, personal well-being, and community impact. By reclaiming time, leaders can strike a healthier balance between their professional responsibilities and their roles as partners, parents, friends, and community members. This chapter explores how intentional time management positively impacts relationships, results, and community well-being, with a special focus on the interplay between professional and personal life.

The Power of Reclaimed Time in Leadership

Educational leadership is demanding, often leaving little energy or time for personal connections and self-care despite the fulfilling nature of the work. However, when leaders reclaim their time through effective delegation, prioritization, and strategic planning, the ripple effects are profound. One of the most meaningful benefits is the ability to deepen relationships. Leaders who are more present and intentional in their interactions can build stronger connections with staff, students, and stakeholders. For example, a principal who delegates administrative tasks can spend more time in classrooms, engaging with teachers and students. This increased visibility fosters trust and creates a sense of shared purpose within the school community.

Reclaimed time also allows leaders to focus on strategic goals that drive systemic change. Shifting from reactive to proactive leadership enables transformational results. A superintendent who reclaims hours previously spent on emails can instead focus on aligning district-wide initiatives, developing innovative programs, or planning for future growth. This dedication to long-term priorities ensures that the district moves forward with clarity and purpose, benefiting both staff and students.

Additionally, effective time management enables leaders to invest in their personal well-being. By carving out space for activities that recharge them—such as exercise, hobbies, or spending time with loved ones—leaders can maintain the resilience and clarity needed to navigate the complexities of their roles. A balanced leader not only is more effective in their professional responsibilities but also serves as a positive role model for staff and students, demonstrating the importance of well-being.

Reclaimed time is more than just a professional asset—it is a personal gift. Leaders who balance work and life effectively bring renewed energy, creativity, and focus to every aspect of their lives, enhancing both their leadership impact and personal relationships.

Personal Example: Balancing Leadership and Family

As a superintendent of a rural district, my professional responsibilities are vast and varied. But outside of work, I am also a wife and the mom of young children. My kids are at an age where quality time with them is not just important—it's irreplaceable. Early in my career, I struggled with the balance, often feeling that my professional demands left me little energy for family life.

As females especially, we carry the emotional load of home. Balancing that with work is particularly challenging for leaders. I became a first-year superintendent when I had my daughter and returned to work when she was only six weeks old. While this is a common challenge for working mothers, it was incredibly difficult to navigate as a new leader. I often felt stretched between two worlds, never feeling fully present in either.

Reclaiming my time as a leader has been integral to being more present for my family. By intentionally prioritizing tasks, delegating responsibilities, and using tools like AI to streamline my work, I've created space to be fully present with my family. I am able to attend most of my children's events and, by planning my evenings carefully, can spend quality time with them while working around their wake times.

The ripple effect is clear: when I'm present and engaged at home, I bring a clearer mind and renewed energy to my role as superintendent. Similarly, when my work is organized and intentional, I can fully enjoy and focus on my personal life. The balance isn't perfect—leadership never stops entirely—but reclaimed time allows me to honor both roles in ways that matter deeply to me and my family.

The Broader Impact of Reclaimed Time

Reclaimed time doesn't just benefit leaders and their families, it creates a positive ripple effect throughout the entire school community. One significant outcome is the strengthening of relationships. When leaders have the time to be present, they can build deeper connections with staff, students, and families. For example, a principal who prioritizes classroom visits and regular staff check-ins fosters a culture of trust and collaboration. These intentional interactions create a more supportive and connected school environment, where everyone feels seen, heard, and valued.

Reclaimed time also drives better results by allowing leaders to focus on high-priority goals. Leaders who dedicate time to strategic initiatives can improve student achievement, increase staff retention, and enhance operational efficiency. A superintendent who uses reclaimed time to align district initiatives with student outcome goals ensures that resources and efforts are directed where they have the greatest impact. This focus not only leads to tangible improvements but also ensures that every decision is intentional and aligned with the district's mission.

Additionally, time saved in leadership roles translates into opportunities for community well-being. Leaders, who have the capacity to engage in outreach, build partnerships, and launch new initiatives can bring valuable resources to their district. For instance, collaborating with local businesses or nonprofits can provide students with unique learning experiences, internships, or additional funding for programs. These partnerships enhance the educational experience and strengthen ties between the school and the broader community.

The ripple effect of reclaimed time is expansive. When leaders are intentional with their time, the benefits extend to everyone they serve, fostering a culture of alignment, trust, and continuous progress.

Strategies for District Leaders

To amplify the ripple effects of reclaimed time, district leaders can implement strategies that benefit students, teachers, and administrators.

For Students

- Student-Centered Programs: Use reclaimed time to invest in initiatives that enhance student experiences, such as mental health resources, extracurricular programs, or academic support. For example, a superintendent might partner with community organizations to bring mental health counselors into schools, addressing a critical need for students.
- Visibility and Engagement: Spend more time engaging directly with students through classroom visits, mentoring, or attending school events. This presence shows students that their voices matter and fosters a stronger connection between leadership and the student body.
- Career Readiness Initiatives: Develop programs that prepare students for life beyond school, such as internships or career exploration opportunities. Leaders who dedicate time to these initiatives provide students with practical skills and a clearer vision for their futures.

For Teachers

- Recognition and Support: Dedicate time to recognizing teachers' hard work through appreciation events, personalized feedback, or professional growth opportunities. A principal who takes time to write handwritten thank-you notes, or host teacher appreciation lunches builds morale and shows genuine gratitude.
- Collaborative Opportunities: Provide teachers with structured time to collaborate and innovate, fostering a culture of shared learning and support. For example, offering weekly PLC sessions allows teachers to share strategies, analyze data, and co-develop solutions to challenges.
- Professional Development: Reclaimed time allows leaders to identify and deliver meaningful professional development tailored to teachers' needs. Workshops on technology integration or culturally responsive teaching can have a significant impact on instructional quality.

For Administrators

- Cross-District Collaboration: Use time savings to facilitate collaboration with other districts, sharing best practices and driving innovation. For example, hosting regional leadership forums can spark new ideas and build a network of support.
- Coaching and Mentorship: Support building administrators by offering regular check-ins, coaching sessions, and opportunities for skill development. Leaders who mentor their teams cultivate stronger, more capable administrators.
- Strategic Planning: Engage in collaborative planning processes that align building-level initiatives with district-wide goals. This alignment ensures that efforts across the district are cohesive and focused on achieving shared priorities.

Honoring Both Roles: Leader and Person

Honoring both the role of a leader and the role of a person is about more than improving professional performance—it is about living a fuller, more intentional life. Effective time management allows educational leaders to balance the demands of their profession with their personal responsibilities, showing up fully in both worlds and giving their best to their districts and their families.

This balance sets an example for others within the school community—teachers, staff, and students alike—that excellence can be pursued without sacrificing personal priorities. Reclaimed time creates space not just for leadership, but for life, and that is where its true power lies.

As this section concludes, it becomes clear that reclaiming time, aligning priorities, and fostering intentional reflection are not merely leadership strategies—they are essential lifelines. In the complex and ever-changing world of educational leadership, the ability to pause, recalibrate, and refocus enables leaders to transcend daily demands and build systems grounded in purpose, clarity, and equity.

The chapters in this part have explored how leaders can regain control of their time, harness technology for efficiency, and empower their teams through strategic delegation. Together, these practices form a foundation for leadership that is both sustainable and impactful. Reclaimed time unlocks the ability to think strategically, act intentionally, and drive meaningful change—not just for schools and districts, but for entire communities.

The ripple effects of intentional leadership extend far beyond the leader. Reclaimed time provides students with access to programs and opportunities that broaden their horizons. It allows teachers to collaborate, innovate, and feel valued for their contributions. It empowers administrators to lead with focus, fostering a culture of alignment and progress across the district. Most importantly, it enables leaders to show up fully—in their professional roles and in their personal lives.

True transformation lies in this balance. Leadership is not about choosing between professional and personal commitments but about finding ways to honor with both intentionality and grace. The stories and strategies shared in this part demonstrate that when leaders reclaim their time and focus on what matters most, they create a legacy of purpose and possibility.

As readers reflect on the practices and principles outlined in this part, they are encouraged to consider what refocus means for their own leadership. What areas need recalibration? Where can time be reclaimed to prioritize high-impact initiatives? How can space be created for reflection and strategic thinking to propel leadership and districts forward?

Refocusing is not a one-time act but a continuous process of evaluation, adjustment, and realignment. It requires courage to step back, commitment to intentionality, and a willingness to lead with both clarity and compassion. The rewards, however, are profound: a stronger team, a thriving school community, and the ability to honor the roles that matter most in leadership and in life.

While this section emphasizes the importance of time, priorities, and reflection for educational leaders, it is ultimately the students who inspire and inform this work. They are the reason for leading, the driving force behind efforts for equity and excellence, and the motivation to continuously improve systems and practices.

As the final part of this book approaches, the focus shifts to the voices of those who matter most: the students. The next section shares reflections from two students on leadership, learning, and their experiences within the educational systems leaders strive to enhance. Their insights serve as a powerful reminder that leadership is not just about policies or practices—it is about the lives touched and the futures shaped.

The journey of refocus is incomplete without the perspectives of those being served. These student voices challenge, inspire, and affirm the importance of intentional, student-centered leadership. Their reflections remind educational leaders that the ultimate measure of their work lies in the success, well-being, and empowerment of their students. Refocus is a powerful tool, but it is also a commitment to continually center leadership on the people and priorities that matter most, guided by the wisdom and aspirations of the students who are privileged to be served.

20 Collective Call to Action

As this journey through *Relationships, Results, and Refocus* comes to a close, the collective voices of Wendy, Rupak, Britney, Aidan, and Zahabu call on educational leaders to carry forward the principles explored within these pages into their schools, districts, and communities. This book has examined the intricacies of educational leadership from multiple perspectives—those at the helm of entire school systems and those whose voices often go unheard: the students. By weaving together these distinct experiences, it highlights that authentic leadership demands partnership, empathy, and an unwavering focus on student needs.

Throughout the book, three essential pillars have repeatedly emerged: building strong relationships, achieving measurable results, and making time to refocus on what truly matters. Readers have seen how a superintendent's deliberate prioritization can ignite district-wide innovation, how a teacher's trust can transform a disengaged learner, and how moments of genuine connection can alter a student's trajectory. Each story—whether from the personal reflections of leaders or the heartfelt words of Aidan and Zahabu—serves as a beacon, illuminating the path through the complexities of modern education.

The true power of this book lies not in its pages but in how its lessons are carried forward. In an era marked by tight budgets, staffing shortages, and shifting policy mandates, it is easy to lose sight of a larger purpose. The approach presented is not a quick fix but a mindset—a conscious choice to see relationships as the cornerstone of every initiative, to hold oneself accountable for real, measurable progress, and to create space for reflection and renewal. These actions ensure that schools become not just institutions of learning, but places of belonging, equity, and hope.

The voices of student authors emphasize that young people are not mere recipients of policies but active partners in shaping their educational journeys. Their stories of triumph, challenge, and perseverance highlight why leadership must be grounded in listening, empathy, and the determination to overcome barriers. Their insights reinforce the central truth of this book: uniting students and leaders in a shared purpose makes educational transformation a tangible reality.

Whether a superintendent making district-wide decisions, a principal fostering a school community, a teacher bridging daily classroom experiences, or a student advocating for change, every individual has a role in this ongoing journey. Each conversation, goal set, and moment of reflection propels the education system toward one that truly sees, hears, and empowers every learner. This collective pursuit of deeper relationships, measurable results, and thoughtful refocus offers the promise of building schools and districts where all voices resonate and where every student's future is a shared commitment fulfilled together.

Bibliography

Anderson, Lorin, and David Krathwohl, eds. *A Taxonomy for Learning, Teaching, and Assessing: A Revision of Bloom's Taxonomy of Educational Objectives.* New York: Longman, 2001.
Bush, Tony. *Theories of Educational Leadership and Management.* 5th ed. London: Sage, 2011.
Center for Promise. "The Impact of Student Engagement on Academic Achievement." 2013.
Education Endowment Foundation. "The Impact of Student Voice on Academic Progress." 2020.
Gallup, Inc. *Gallup Student Poll: The State of Student Engagement.* Gallup Press Report, 2018.
Gronn, Peter. "Distributed Leadership as a Unit of Analysis." *The Leadership Quarterly* 14, no. 4 (2003): 423–51.
Harvard Business Review. "The Impact of Organizational Alignment on Performance." Harvard Business Review, April 2008.
Heifetz, Ronald A. *Leadership without Easy Answers.* Cambridge, MA: Belknap Press of Harvard University Press, 1994.
Kouzes, James M., and Barry Z. Posner. *The Leadership Challenge: How to Make Extraordinary Things Happen in Organizations.* 5th ed. San Francisco, CA: Jossey-Bass, 2017.
Leithwood, Kenneth, and Doris Jantzi. "Transformational School Leadership Effect on Student Achievement." In *The School Effect: Implications of School Leadership*, edited by Kenneth Leithwood et al., 31–66. New York: Teachers College Press, 2004.
Leithwood, Kenneth, and Karen Seashore Louis. "Linking Leadership to Student Learning: The Contributions of Leader Efficacy." *Educational Administration Quarterly* 38, no. 4 (2002): 496–528.
McChesney, Chris, Sean Covey, and Jim Huling. *The 4 Disciplines of Execution: Achieving Your Wildly Important Goals.* New York: Free Press, 2012.
McKinsey & Company. "The Value of Well-Defined Strategic Roles." *McKinsey Quarterly*, 2009.

National Education Association. *Importance of School Climate*. Washington, DC: National Education Association, 2013.

Northouse, Peter G. *Leadership: Theory and Practice*. 8th ed. Thousand Oaks, CA: SAGE Publications, 2019.

Senge, Peter M. *The Fifth Discipline: The Art and Practice of the Learning Organization*. New York: Doubleday, 1990.

Spillane, James P., John B. Diamond, and Nancy F. Hopkins. *Distributed Leadership in Practice*. New York: Teachers College Press, 2007.

University of Minnesota, Center for Applied Research and Educational Improvement. "Enhancing Educational Outcomes: A Guide for Schools." 2010.

University of Washington, Center for Educational Leadership. "Student Voice and Engagement in Schools." 2015.

YouthTruth. "Student Engagement and Leadership Report." 2018.